an Out of Joint and Octagon Theatre Bolton co-production

This May Hurt A B

a play by Stella Feehily

Touring 2014

6-15 March
Theatre Royal, Bury St Edmunds

25 March – 5 April
Octagon Theatre Bolton

8-12 April
Traverse Theatre, Edinburgh

15-19 April
Everyman Theatre Cheltenham

22-26 April
Oxford Playhouse

30 April – 3 May
Bristol Old Vic

7-10 May
Liverpool Playhouse

14 May – 21 June
St. James Theatre, London

London performances presented by Karl Sydow

Cast:

Stephanie Cole	Iris
Brian Protheroe	Nicholas, Prime Minister
Hywel Morgan	Aneurin Bevan, Danny, Terry, Archie
Tristram Wymark	Winston Churchill, Mr Weaver, Roger, John, Milton
Jane Wymark	Mariel, The NHS
Frances Ashman	Tabitha, Dinah, Bea, Dr Gray
William Hope	Hank, Miles, Sam, The Grim Reaper
Natalie Klamar	Gina, Cassandra, Aly, Wendy

Director **Max Stafford-Clark**
Set & Costume Designer **Tim Shortall**
Lighting Designer **Jason Taylor**
Sound Designer **Andy Smith**
Associate Director **Tim Hoare**
Choral Composer **Adam Pleeth**
Soundtrack Composer **Charlotte Hatherley**
Choreographer **Orian Michaeli**
Assistant Director **Maureen A. Bryan**
Casting Associate **Leila Bertrand**

Production Manager **Gary Beestone**
Company Stage Manager **Elaine Yeung**
Deputy Stage Manger **Kerry Sullivan**
Assistant Stage Manager **Laura Smith**
Costume Supervisor **Biddy Guy**
Re-lighter **Andy Furby**
Set Construction **Footprint Scenery Ltd**
Production Photography **John Haynes**
PR **James Lever** for Target Live

This production is supported by **Frank and Elizabeth Brenan**

Special thanks to JJ McConnell

With thanks to Hampstead Theatre, Caroline Heale at Guildford School of Acting, Royal Surrey Hospital, Munir and Clinical Engineering at The Royal London Hospital, Guildford Shakespeare Company, Salisbury Playhouse, GSMD

out of joint

Inquisitive, epic, authentic and original: Out of Joint is a national and international touring theatre company, developing entertaining theatre that broadens horizons and investigates our times.

Under the direction of Max Stafford-Clark, who co-founded the company in 1993 following his artistic directorship of the Royal Court, Out of Joint has premiered plays from leading writers including April De Angelis, Sebastian Barry, Richard Bean, Alistair Beaton, Caryl Churchill, David Hare, Robin Soans and Timberlake Wertenbaker, as well as launching first-time writers such as Mark Ravenhill and Stella Feehily.

Touring all over the UK, Out of Joint frequently performs at and co-produces with key venues such as the Royal Court and the National Theatre. The company has performed in six continents, and its recent production of *Our Country's Good* will tour overseas in 2014. Back home, Out of Joint also pursues an extensive education programme, which recently explanded to include not only work with education establishments but also writing and devising courses for participants of all ages.

This Summer and Autumn, Out of Joint will collaborate with Chichester Festival Theatre and Shakespeare's Globe on a new play by Richard Bean, *Pitcairn*.

Director: **Max Stafford-Clark**
Producer: **Panda Cox**
Associate Producer: **Graham Cowley**
Marketing Manager: **Jon Bradfield**
Company Administrator: **Martin Derbyshire**
PA & Education Administrator: **Isabel Quinzaños**
Finance Officer: **Sandra Rapley**

Board of Directors Linda Bassett, John Blackmore (Chair), Guy Chapman, Elyse Dodgson, Iain Gillie, Stephen Jeffreys, Paul Jesson, James Jones, Danny Sapani, Karl Sydow.

Out of Joint
7 Thane Works, London N7 7NU
Tel: 020 7609 0207
Email: ojo@outofjoint.co.uk
Web: www.outofjoint.co.uk

KEEP IN TOUCH
For information on our shows, tour details and offers, get in touch as above, or join our mailing list via our website. We are also on Twitter and Facebook.

EDUCATION
Out of Joint offers a diverse programme of workshops and discussions for groups coming to see our performances, as well writing courses. For full details of our education programme, resource packs or workshops, contact Isabel at Out of Joint.

Out of Joint is grateful to the following for their support over the years: Arts Council England, The Foundation for Sport and the Arts, The Granada Foundation, Yorkshire Bank Charitable Trust, The Baring Foundation, The Paul Hamlyn Foundation, The Olivier Foundation, The Peggy Ramsay Foundation, The John S Cohen Foundation, The David Cohen Charitable Trust, The National Lottery through the Arts Council of England, The Prudential Awards, Stephen Evans, Karl Sydow, Friends of Theatre, John Lewis Partnership, Unity Theatre Trust, Royal Victoria Hall Foundation, Harold Hyam Wingate Foundation, Elizabeth and Frank Brenan. Out of Joint is a Registered Charity No. 1033059

Supported using public funding by
ARTS COUNCIL ENGLAND
LOTTERY FUNDED

Opposite page: Bang Bang Bang *by Stella Feehily, photo by John Haynes.*
Above: Top Girls *by Caryl Churchill in rehearsal, photo by Manuel Harlan;*
Right: Shopping and Fucking *by Mark Ravenhill and* The Big Fellah *by Richard Bean, photos by John Haynes.*

FRIENDS OF OUT OF JOINT

Out of Joint is hugely grateful to our Friends, whose support is increasingly important in enabling us to make and tour ambitious theatre.

The Friends Scheme is an affordable way to support us and become more involved with our work - you might even decide to contribute to a specific project. *Our heartfelt thanks to:*

Kate Ashfield
Linda Bassett
Richard Bean
Alistair Beaton
John Blackmore
Danny Boyle
Frank & Elizabeth Brenan
David Brooks
Anthony Burton
Rachel Chambers
Guy Chapman
Chipo Chung
Jeremy Conway
Ron Cook
Dominic Cooke
Peter & Angela Cox

Eastwell Manor
Elyse Dodgson
Josephine Fenton
Roy Foster
Friends of Theatre
Iain Gillie
Richard & Mary Gillie
Edwina Grosvenor
Mr & Mrs Harter
Andy Herrity
Roland Jaquarello
Paul Jesson
James Jones
Mary Kerr & Roger Boden
Lord Kinnock
Rebecca Lenkiewicz

Michael & Jill Lewis
Philida Lloyd
Cameron Mackintosh
Amanda Mccleary
Ian McKellan
Juliet Meinrath
Ali Ostrer
David Owen Norris
Ian Redford
Alan Rickman
David Rintoul
Max Stafford-Clark
Tom Stoppard
Ripley Talbot
Richard Wilson

To be involved, call us on 020 7609 0207
or email Martin@outofjoint.co.uk

ONLINE BOOKSHOP
Visit Out of Joint's online shop to buy play scripts and theatre books at discounted prices.
www.outofjoint.co.uk

octagon
Bolton

"The most intimate and atmospheric theatre-in-the-round in the country"
Maxine Peake on the Octagon Theatre Bolton

Critically Acclaimed Theatre: The Octagon believes in the finest standard of theatre. We produce an annual season of productions that include Shakespeare, American drama, great European plays and contemporary classics alongside new plays, musicals, plays for family audiences and plays that are rooted in the culture of Bolton and the North West.

New Writing: The Octagon is committed to cultivating new artists and audiences for theatre through our continued development of new plays and writers. The Octagon regularly brings world premiere productions to the main stage and continues to develop emerging local talent through its thriving new writing department.

Creative Partnerships: Through numerous tours and co-productions the Octagon's work has been seen all over the country. The Octagon's 2012 co-production of *Our Country's Good* will also reach international audiences as it tours to America later this year.

Together with principal sponsor, the University of Bolton, the Octagon works to develop a significant strategic approach to creativity and learning in the region, with a commitment to supporting the development of future talent.

In the Community: The Octagon Learning and Participation Department provides a stimulating and challenging participatory community resource for over 20,000 people every year.

Hobson's Choice, photo by Ian Tilton

Visit Us: The Octagon has recently undergone a major renovation to modernise the auditorium and refurbish the front of house areas, including a brand new café, kitchen and bar, as well as a new food and drink offer based on locally sourced, seasonal produce.

Chief Executive: Roddy Gauld
Artistic Director: David Thacker

Octagon Theatre
Howell Croft South, Bolton
BL1 1SB

Box Office: 01204 520661
www.octagonbolton.co.uk

Registered Charity Number 248833

FRANCES ASHMAN

Frances trained at the Guildhall School of Music & Drama. She appeared in Out of Joint and Octagon Theate Bolton's *Bang Bang Bang* (with Leicester Curve, Royal Court and Salisbury Playhouse). Other **theatre** work includes *Our Ajax* (Southwark Playhouse); *People* (National Theatre); *After the Accident* (Soho Theatre); *Bang Bang Bang* (Royal Court); *Pornography* (Birmingham Rep & Tricycle); *In The Blood* (Finborough Theatre); *Cockroach* (National Theatre of Scotland); *Zuva Crumbling* (Lyric Hammersmith); and *Macbett, Pericles* and *The Winter's Tale* (all RSC). On **television** Frances has been seen in *Mayday, The Reckoning, Doctor Who, Law and Order UK, Missing, Trial & Retribution* and *Gunrush*.

STEPHANIE COLE

Stephanie trained at Bristol Old Vic Theatre School (1958/9) and her first professional role, at the age of 17, was as a 90 year old in a play with Leonard Rossiter at Bristol Old Vic. Stephanie's other **theatre** includes *Pygmalion, Separate Tables, Whom Do I Have the Honour of Addressing?, Driving Miss Daisy* (Chichester Festival Theatre); *Born In The Gardens, The Rivals* (Theatre Royal and tour); *Blithe Spirit* (Savoy Theatre, West End); *The Shell Seekers* (Tour); *A Passionate Woman* (Comedy Theatre, West End, nominated for an Evening Standard Award); *Quartet* (Albery Theatre, West End); *Steel Magnolias* (Lyric Theatre); *Rose* (Duke of Yorks Theatre); *Noises Off* (Savoy Theatre); *The Relapse* (Old Vic); and tours of *So Long Life* and *Equally Divided*. **Television** includes *Open All Hours* and *Still Open All Hours, Coronation Street* (Best Comedy Performance, British Soap Awards 2012), *The Lady Vanishes, George & Bernard Shaw*, 4 series of *Doc Martin, Midsomer Murders, Housewife 49, Born and Bred, Back Home, Life As We Know It*, 2 series of *Keeping Mum*, 4 series of *Waiting for God* (Best Comedy Actress, British Comedy Awards 1990), *In The Cold Light of Day, Memento Mori*, 2 series of *A Bit of a Do, Talking Heads: Soldiering On, The Return of the Antelope*, 3 series of *Tenko, Going Gently*. **Film** includes *Miss Pettigrew Lives for a Day, Grey Owl, Torquay Summer, That Week In Nempnett Thrubwell, International Velvet*. **Radio** includes *Cabin Pressure* (4 series), *Martha's Metamorphosis, Ed Reardon's Week* (9 Series), *Latvian Angel/The Evening, The Tank Man & Perfect Wood* - readings for several Bath Festivals for Radio 4, *Poetry Please, Book of the Week, Book at Bedtime*. Extensive audio recordings include the *Miss Marple* Series and *Woman's Hour Books*. Stephanie's autobiography entitled *A Passionate Life* was published in 1998. In 2005 she was awarded the OBE for Services to Drama, Mental Health and the Elderly. She is a member of the Board of the Royal Theatrical Fund.

WILLIAM HOPE

William's **theatre** includes: *The Seven Year Itch* (Queens Theatre); *All My Sons* (West Yorkshire Playhouse); *Doctor of Honour* (Cheek By Jowl); *The False Servant* (Gate Theatre); *Twelfth Night* (Sheffield Crucible); *The Normal Heart* (Royal Court/ Noel Coward) *The Cherry Orchard*, *Soul of the White Ant*, *The Lower Depths*, *La Ronde* (Manchester Royal Exchange); *Live From Golgotha* (Drill Hall); *Miss Julie* (Phoenix Theatre); *Double Cross* (Theatre Royal, Windsor); *PVT Wars* (Latchmere); *Antony and Cleopatra*; *The Way of the World* (Nottingham Playhouse); *Swim Visit* (Donmar Warehouse); *The Foreigner* (Noel Coward); *The Country Wife*, *Long Day's Journey Into Night* (Leicester Haymarket); *'Tis Pity She's a Whore*, *As You Like It*, *Macbeth*, *Medea* (Northcott Theatre); *Zoo Story*, *Troilus and Cressida* (National Arts Theatre); *Washroom* (Almost Free Theatre). **Film** includes *Walking with the Enemy*, *Dark Shadows*, *The Lady*, *Captain America: The First Avenger*, *The Whistleblower*, *Cold Fusion*, *Spiders*, *Dark Floors*, *Legacy*, *Sherlock Holmes*, *The Walker*, *Trade Routes*, *The Detonator*, *The Marksman*, *Finding Rin Tin Tin*, *Submerged*, *XXX*, *Sky Captain & The World of Tomorrow*, *Labyrinth*, *McLibel*, *Obedience*, *Going Home*, *The Saint*, *Shining Through*, *Hellbound: Hellraiser II*, *Aliens*, *The Last Days of Patton*, *The Lords of Discipline*. **Television** includes *Thomas the Tank Engine*, *Shall We Kiss* (HBO), *Burton and Taylor*, *Marple: Endless Night*, *Upstairs, Downstairs*, *Spooks* (series 10), *Episodes*, *The Last Days of Lehman Brothers*, *Moonshot*, *Holby City*, *Bonekickers*, *Lewis*, *Midsomer Murders*, *9/11: The Twin Towers*, *Avengers*, *Ultimate Force*, *Broken News*, *The Eagle Falls*, *Egypt*, *Viva Liberty*, *Dunkirk*, *Gimme Gimme Gimme*, *Drop The Dead Donkey*, *Sword of Honour*, *As Time Goes By*, *92 Grsovenor Street*, *Behind Enemy Lines*, *The Shell Seekers*, *The Vanishing Man*, *To Save The Children*. **Radio**: William was a member of the BBC Radio Rep 1982-83 and is frequently heard on the BBC and in independent productions. He also regularly records audio books. **Directing**: *2012 - A Fairy Tale* (Queens's College London)

NATALIE KLAMAR

Natalie Trained At LAMDA. **Theatre** includes *All's Well That Ends Well*, *As You Like It*, *Hamlet*, *A Soldier In Every Son – The Rise Of The Aztecs*, *King John* and *Richard III* (all Royal Shakespeare Company); *Sense* (Hen & Chickens Theatre); *Town* (Royal & Derngate, Northampton); *Breakfast At Tiffany's* (Theatre Royal Haymarket) and *The Exquisite Corpse* (Southwark Playhouse). **Television** includes *Midsomer Murders*, *Misfits* and *Doctors*. **Film** includes *Harry Potter and the Philosopher's Stone*.

HYWEL MORGAN

Hywel is a Welsh-speaking Cardiffian who trained at Rose Bruford College of Speech and Drama. **Theatre** credits include: *A Walk on Part: The Fall of New Labour* (Live Theatre/Soho Theatre); *War & Peace, Mill on the Floss* (Shared Experience); *ONA$$I$* (Chichester); *Surviving Spike, Our Man in Havana* (Bill Kenwright); *Indian Ink* (Salisbury Playhouse); *Kind Hearts & Coronets, A Man for All Seasons* - Leon Sinden Award (Pitlochry Festival Theatre); *The Importance of Being Earnest, To Reach the Clouds, Feelgood, Because It's There* and *A Midsummer Night's Dream* (Nottingham Playhouse); *Blithe Spirit* and *Dancing at Lughnasa* (The Watermill) and *Football* (Made in Wales). Other theatre includes: *Vanity Fair, The Rivals, A Christmas Carol, Small Change, Time of my Life, Julius Cæsar, Henry V* and *Romeo & Juliet*. **Film** includes *Page Eight* (David Hare), *W.E.* (Madonna) *The End of the Fucking World* and *Me, Me, Me* which won the Golden Dragon at the Newport Film Festival. **Television** includes: *The Tunnel, Talking to the Dead, Skins, Da Vinci's, Demons, Casualty, Doctors, Family, EastEnders, Pobol y Cwm, Dark Matters* and *Get Out Alive*. **Radio** includes *After Eden, The Mark of Zorro* and *Letters to Mam* (Radio 4) and various episodes of *Doctor Who* for Big Finish.

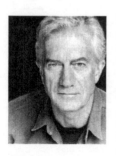

BRIAN PROTHEROE

Brian appeared in Out of Joint's *The Convicts' Opera, Three Sisters, Break of Day* and *Some Explicit Polaroids*, and in Octagon Theatre Bolton's *An Inspector Calls* and *Long Day's Journey Into Night*. Other **theatre** includes *Broken Glass* (Tricycle Theatre/ Vaudeville, West End); *Moonlight and Magnolias* (Watermill, Newbury); *Noises Off, Home Truths* (Birmingham Rep); *The Lord of the Rings* (West End); *The Birthday Party* (Bristol Old Vic); title role in *Macbeth* (Derby Playhouse); *Losing Louis* (Hampstead and West End); *The Price* (Act UK Tour); *The Cherry Orchard, Penny for a Song* (Oxford Stage Company); *The Tempest, The Winters Tale, Pericles* (RSC); *Aladdin, Cinderella* (Stratford East); *Relatively Speaking* (UK tour); *The Wood Demon* (Playhouse Theatre); *Hamlet* (Greenwich tour); *The Sisters Rosensweig* (Old Vic); *Lysistrata* (Wyndhams, West End); *The Taming of the Shrew, Who's Afraid of Virginia Wolf* (West Yorkshire Playhouse); *Schippel the Plumber* (Greenwich); *Pump Boys & Dinettes* (Piccadilly, West End); *The Iceman Cometh, Long Voyage Home, Larkrise to Candleford, Dispatches* (National Theatre); *Leave Him To Heaven* (New London); **Television** includes *Whitechapel, Casualty, Spooks, Love Soup, Holby City, Dr Willoughby, Gentlemen & Players, To Have and to Hold, Reilly Ace of Spies,* Titus *Andronicus, Henry VI* and *Richard III*. **Film** appearances include *The Biggest Bank Robbery* and *Superman*. Brian has combined his acting with a **music** career and has also composed music for a number of pantomimes at the Theatre Royal, Stratford East, London.

JANE WYMARK

Jane's **theatre** includes: Narrator for *My First Sleeping Beauty* and *My First Cinderella* (English National Ballet); *Racing Demon* (Sheffield Crucible); *All My Sons* (York Theatre Royal); *The House Of Mirth* (Workshop, Cambridge Theatre Co); *Sixteen Words for Water* (Old Red Lion); *Game, Set and Match* (London Toast Theatre, Copenhagen); *A Woman's Place* - One Woman Show (Dhaka, Bangladesh); *Short Sharp Shock* (Royal Court and Stratford East); *The Streets of London* (Stratford East and West End); *Hamlet* (Old Vic/World Tour); *Three Sisters* (Watford Palace Theatre); *Twelfth Night* , *Ivanov* (Prospect Theatre Co); *A Man for All Seasons*, *When We Are Married*, *The Importance of Being Earnest*, *Equus*, *Arms and the Man* (Birmingham Rep); *The Loonies* (Hampstead Theatre Club); *The Churchill Play*, *Loot*, *The Taming of the Shrew*, *Three Sisters*, *Brassneck* (Nottingham Playhouse); *Boys Into Men* and *Home Truths*, *A Reasonable Percentage*, *Love from the Prodigal*, *The Twenty Second Day*. Jane is best known on **television** as Joyce Barnaby in *Midsomer Murders*. Other TV includes *Doctors*, *Sinchronicity*, *Underworld*, *The Peter Principle*, *Rob Roy*, *Pie In The Sky*, *No Bananas*, *Giving Tongue*, *Screen Two: A Landing on the Sun*, *Lovejoy*, *Calling The Shots*, *Maigret*, *Tell Tale Hearts*, *Between The Lines*, *Seconds Out*, *Bhangra Girls*, *Fatal Inversion*, *Chalkface*, *Children Of The North*, *The Sidmouth Letters*, *Best of Friends*, *Beasts*, *Poldark*, *The Bass Player and the Blonde*, *Fathers and Families*, *Rooms*. **Film** includes *All Men Are Mortal*, *The Fool*.

TRISTRAM WYMARK

Tristram's **theatre** includes *Collaborators*, *Much Ado About Nothing*, *Richard III*, *Anna's Room*, *The Duchess of Malfi*, *The Critic* (National Theatre); *Cause Celebre* (Old Vic); *Pygmalion* (Chichester Festival Theatre), *Phaedra* (National Theatre and US Tour); *David Copperfield* (Mercury Theatre); *The Fastest Clock in the Universe* (Naach Theatre Company); *The Hot Zone* (Conspirators Kitchen, BAC); *Backpackers Orpheus* (Sound Theatre); *Nothing* (East 59th Street Theatre); *David Copperfield* (West Yorkshire Playhouse); *Hamlet* (Thelma Holt No 1 Tour); *Wild Sargasso Sea*, *The Cherry Orchard*, *Dance of Death*, *Mozart's Nachtmusik*, *Two Way Mirror*, *Pal Joey*, *Macbeth*, *The Millionairess*, *Widowers Houses*, *Hamlet*, *The Bar of a Tokyo Hotel*, *'Tis Pity She's A Whore*, *Phaedra*, *A Tale of Two Cities*, *Enrico IV*, *Mrs Warren's Profession* (Glasgow Citizen's Theatre); *The Tempest* (Thelma Holt No 1 Tour); *Semi-Monde* (Lyric Theatre, West End); *Lady Windemere's Fan* (Triumph Apollo); *A Midsummer Night's Dream* (New Shakespeare Co). **Television** includes *Lucan*, *Call The Midwife*, *Eastenders*, *Midsomer Murders*, *Getting Out Alive*, *Hollyoaks*, *Joe's Palace*, *Hustle 4*, *Naval Officer*, *Ghost Ship*, *Kavanagh QC*, *Sharpe*, *Jenny's War*, *Thin Air*, *Victoria Wood Play*, *Haggard*, *Mrs Warren's Profession*. **Film** includes *The Cold Room* (Cold Room Productions); *Good & Bad At Games* (Portman Quintet); *Another Country* (Castlezone Ltd)

MAUREEN A. BRYAN - Assistant Director
Maureen worked closely with founding members Ron Silver, Susan Sarandon and Alec Baldwin, in the early years of The Creative Coalition (TCC) in New York. She received a Master of Fine Arts degree in directing from The Actors Studio, where she studied directing with Arthur Penn, Mark Rydell and others. Her first 16mm film titled *Behind Closed Doors* was shot in New York and subsequent directing credits include *Faces of Hope* for ABC Networks, featuring Malcolm McDowell, Annabella Sciorra, Peter Gallagher and others. She directed *The Legends of Women from Blues* – featuring Chaka Khan and other music videos. Maureen's theatre directing credits include *Orphans* by Lyle Kessler; *Fences* by August Wilson; *The Gingham Dog* by Lanford Wilson and *Journey of the Griots: Souls Unsold* which she wrote and directed. Maureen founded The Voice Of A Woman, which shares the creativity, stories and experiences of women globally.

LEILA BERTRAND - Casting Associate
Leila's **theatre** work includes *One Monkey Don't Stop No Show* (Tour, Albany Deptford); The Chairs, The Good Solider (Bath Theatre Royal); Fragile Land (Hampstead Theatre/Theatre Royal Stratford East); Paradise Bound, The Wedding Dance (Nitro); Macbeth (Out of Joint); Black Crow (Clean Break); Fly (Liverpool Everyman); *Blithe Spirit, Major of Zalamaea, The Entertainer* (Liverpool PlayHouse/Everyman); *The Deep Blue Sea* (Liverpool Everyman) *Suddenly Last Summer* , *Rats Buckets and Bombs* (Nottingham Play House). **Film** Includes: *Free Style, Play Hard, Collusion, The Bird Can't Fly, Toy Boys, Foot Ball* and *Long Time Dead*.

PANDA COX - Producer
Panda joined Out of Joint in 2009 as PA to Max Stafford-Clark, and became Deputy Producer in 2011. Independently she has produced *Tu I Teraz* (Here and Now) at Hampstead Theatre and Colchester Mercury Theatre earlier this year; and Jessica Swale's production of *The Palace of the End* for Red Handed at the Arcola in 2010. She was previously producer for Dancing Brick, and has worked with Escalator East to Edinburgh, Latitude Festival, and Norfolk & Norwich Festival.

STELLA FEEHILY - Writer
Stella's short play *Game* was commissioned by Fishamble Theatre Company and premiered at the Project Arts Centre, Dublin. Her plays for Out of Joint include *Duck* (co-produced with the Royal Court), *O Go My Man* (with the Royal Court; joint winner of the 2007 Susan Smith Blackburn Award); *Dreams of Violence* (with Soho Theatre); and *Bang Bang Bang* (with Leicester Curve, Octagon Theatre Bolton, the Royal Court and Salisbury Playhouse). *Catch*, written with four other female playwrights, opened at the Royal Court in December 2006. Stella's radio plays include Sweet Bitter (Lyric FM) and Julia Roberts Teeth (Radio 3). As an actress, work includes The Seagull (Culture Project - The Lynn Redgrave Theatre, New York); *A Christmas Carol* (Gate Theatre, Dublin); *Macbeth* (Tivoli Theatre); *Ten* (Project Arts Centre); *Letters to Felice* (Pavilion Theatre); and *Iphigenia At Aulis* (Abbey Theatre). TV and film credits include *Fair City, Ballykissangel* and *The Ambassador*. Stella worked as Assistant Director on *The Overwhelming* (Roundabout Theatre, New York) and *The Convicts' Opera* (Out of Joint/Sydney Theatre Company).

CHARLOTTE HATHERLEY - Soundtrack Composer

Charlotte Hatherley is a songwriter, multi-instrumentalist, producer and composer. She has released 3 solo albums: *Grey Will Fade*, *The Deep Blue* and *New Worlds* and has also performed in various bands, most notably Ash and Bat For Lashes. The first EP from her most recent project, Sylver Tongue, was released to critical acclaim in late 2012. The album is due for release in 2014.

TIM HOARE - Associate Director

Tim is currently an associate director at Out of Joint and a staff director at the National Theatre, assisting Sam Mendes on King Lear. He was co-founder and Artistic Director of Chichester Festival Theatre's "Festival on the Fly", a temporary venue celebrating CFT's 50th season, for which he directed the world premiere of Penelope Skinner's play *Fred's Diner*. Other directing work includes *What People Do* (Old Vic Tunnels/Viscera Theatre); *Yes, Prime Minister* (redirection of a production by Jonathan Lynn, CFT and national tour); *Number 1* (Bush Theatre); *Henry V* Trafalgar Studios/National Theatre Tbilisi, Georgia); Bash (Barons Court Theatre). As an associate and assistant director, work for Chichester Festival Theatre includes *South Downs* and *The Browning Version* (transferring to the Harold Pinter Theatre, West End), *Top Girls* (Out of Joint, tour and Trafalgar Studios), *Alice in Wonderland*, *The Master Builder*, *Pygmalion* and *Yes, Prime Minister*; and *Eigengrau* (Bush Theatre); *Slaves* (Theatre 503).

ORIAN MICHAELI - Choreographer

Stage work includes *To The Past* (choreographer/dancer, Israeli Reality Festival Jerusalem, Acco Theatre, Tmuna Theatre Tel-Aviv); *Lady Dog* by Iris Marko (dancer/deviser; Tmuna Theatre Tel-Aviv, Suzan Dalal Theatre Tel-Aviv); *Glory Monster* by Michal Herman (dancer/deviser, Klipa Theatre Tel-Aviv, Beit Tami Tel-Aviv, Tiberius Cultural Centre, Eilat Cultural Centre, Yavne Theatre); Klipa Theatre's *The Observatory* (actress/dancer/acrobat, The Israel Festival 2011, Tbilisi International Theatre Festival); *DayDreams* by Meirav Cohen (dancer/ deviser, Acco Festival, Nahmani Theatre Tel-Aviv, Suzan Dalal Theatre Tel-Aviv, Acco Theatre); *Treasures In The Wall* by Haled Abu Ali (actress, Acco Theatre); *Talented Like A Demon* (Choreographer/dancer, Jewish Summer Festival Budapest, Red Shell Festival Tel-Aviv, Acco Theatre); *Waiting for Zoro* by Yaara Perah (actress/deviser, Klipa Theatre Tel-Aviv); *The Tired Hero* by Moni Yosef (actress /choreographer, Acco Theatre); *Biaur* by Ido Tadmor Osnat Shnek Yosef and Smadar Yaaron (dancer/deviser, Acco Festival in Collaboration with Acco Theatre and Suzan Dalal Theatre); *Ballad of the Burning Star* (choreographer, deviser, actress, Theatre Ad Infinitum). Screen work includes *Goose Pumps* (Winner of the Friendly Crowd Award, Southern Cinema Festival), *It's Not All That Simple* and *Fairy on the Roof* (Winner of the First Prize Award at the Apus Festival Tel-Aviv). Orian won the Keren Sharet Foundation Scolarship and the Lohamei Hagetaot Museum Award.

ADAM PLEETH - Choral Composer

Adam has composed and performed music for *The Elephantom* (National Theatre Shed); *Ballad of the Burning Star* (Theatre Ad Infinitum); *Juana in a Million*; and *The Adventures of Curious Ganz* (Silent Tide). As a composer, projects include *Entries on Love* and *Time Stands Still When I Think of You*. Work as a musician includes *Brief Encounter* (Kneehigh); *Cinderella* (Travelling Light); and *Babel* (Wildworks).

TIM SHORTALL - Set and Costume Designer

Designs for Out of Joint and Max Stafford-Clark include: *Our Country's Good* (25th anniversary production with Octagon Theatre Bolton, then at St. James's Theatre), *Top Girls* (Chichester Festival Theatre and Trafalgar Studios), *The Big Fellah* (Lyric Hammersmith) and *The Overwhelming* (National Theatre and Roundabout NYC). Other highlights include: *La Cage Aux Folles* directed by Terry Johnson (West End and Broadway – 2010 Tony nomination for Best Scenic Design of a Musical); *A New World – The Life of Thomas Paine* (Shakespeare's Globe); *The Philanthropist* directed by David Grindley with Simon Russell Beale (Donmar Warehouse) and Matthew Broderick (Broadway); *Awake and Sing* directed by Michael Attenborough with Stockard Channing (Almeida), *Sweet Charity* (Menier Chocolate Factory and Theatre Royal Haymarket); *Whipping It Up*, *Elton John's Glasses*, *See How They Run*, *Telstar*, *Body and Soul* (all West End); *Old Money*, and *Race* both directed by Terry Johnson (Hampstead); *900 Oneonta* (Old Vic); *Disappeared* (Royal Court); *Privates On Parade*, *The Colonel Bird* and *Broken Glass* (all directed by Rupert Goold). Dance includes: new works for Sadler's Wells Royal Ballet, Scottish Ballet, Norwegian National Ballet and Dutch National Ballet. TMA award nomination *Roots* & RAI Prize/Prix Italia *The Nightingale*. Future designs include Richard Bean's new play *Pitcairn* directed by Max Stafford-Clark (for Out of Joint at Chichester Festival Theatre and Shakespeare's Globe).

ANDY SMITH - Sound Designer

Andy is Chief Electrician and resident sound designer at The Octagon Theatre Bolton. Over the last 12 years he has designed over 100 shows and musicals, and has seen his work tour all over the UK and Europe. He has collaborated with Out of Joint on the world premieres of *Mixed up North* and *Bang Bang Bang*, which enjoyed a successful tour around the UK and a sold out run at the Royal Court Theatre Upstairs. Most recently he was sound designer on the hugely successful co-production and tour of *Our Country's Good*, which is due to tour again in 2014 in the UK and USA. Andy always enjoys working with Out of Joint and looks forward to creating another excellent production.

MAX STAFFORD-CLARK - Director

Max is Out of Joint's Artistic Director, and a former Artistic Director of Royal Court Theatre and the Traverse Theatre, as well as co-founder of Joint Stock Theatre Group. World Premieres include: *Top Girls*, *Serious Money*, *Shopping and Fucking*, *Rita, Sue and Bob Too*, and plays by Richard Bean, April De Angelis, David Hare, Timberlake Wertenbaker, Stephen Jeffreys, Sebastian Barry, Howard Brenton, Sue Townsend, Alistair Beaton, Jim Cartwright, Stella Feehily, Robin Soans and many more. Acclaimed revivals of classics include: *Three Sisters*, *King Lear*, *She Stoops to Conquer*, *Macbeth*. Max has directed for the RSC, National Theatre, Sydney Theatre Company, and New York's Roundabout Theatre and Public Theatre and most recently Culture Project, where he directed *The Seagull* in 2013. Several of his productions have transferred to the West End, including *Our Country's Good*, *Feelgood*, *Top Girls* and *Serious Money*. His publications include *Letters to George*, *Taking Stock*, *Our Country's Good: Page to Stage* and the recently published *Journal of the Plague Year*.

KARL SYDOW - Producer, London

Productions planned this year include international tours of the centennial production of *Under Milk Wood*, directed by Terry Hands and featuring the Tony Award-winner Owen Teale; Out of Joint & Octagon Theatre Bolton's *Our Country's Good*; and *The Last Confession* with David Suchet. Karl's **UK credits** include *Backbeat* (Citizens Theatre, Glasgow & The Duke of York's, London); *The Line* by Timberlake Wertenbaker; *Memory* by Johnathan Lichtenstein; *Triptych* by Edna O'Brien; *Ring Round the Moon* by Jean Anouilh and adapted by Christopher Fry directed by Sean Mathias (Playhouse); *Jenufa* by Timberlake Wertenbaker directed by Irina Brown (Arcola); *Dirty Dancing* (Aldwych Theatre, London, which achieved the largest advance sales in the history of the West End); the London & Sydney production of *Dance of Death* with Sir Ian McKellen, Francis de la Tour and Owen Teale; *And Then There Were None* by Agatha Christie; Bea Arthur (Savoy); *Auntie and Me* (Wyndham's); *Michael Moore, Live!* at the Roundhouse; the West End premiere of Noel Coward's *Semi Monde*; *Mouth to Mouth* (Albery); *Speed the Plow*; *Drummers* by Simon Bennet and *Some Explicit Polaroids* by Mark Ravenhill, both directed by Max Stafford-Clark for Out of Joint; *Macbeth* with Rufus Sewell (Queens Theatre); *A Swell Party - a celebration of Cole Porter* (Vaudeville); Timberlake Wertenbaker's *Our Country's Good* (6 Tony nominations, New York Critics Award Best Foreign Play and Olivier Award Best Play); *Hysteria* (Best Comedy, Olivier Awards); and an adaptation of Sue Townsend's novel *The Queen and I* which was Out of Joint's inaugural production. **Broadway credits** include: *Backbeat*; *The Seagull* featuring Kristin Scott Thomas; *All My Sons* with Katie Holmes; *American Buffalo*; *Our Country's Good*. Other New York credits include: *Haunted* by Edna O'Brien featuring Brenda Blethyn; *Terra Haute* by Edmond White; and at BAM the NT's production of *Happy Days* by Samuel Beckett featuring Fiona Shaw, directed by Deborah Warner. Karl was a founder member and continues to serve on the board of Out of Joint. **Film**: Karl also served as a director of Renaissance Film Company. Renaissance productions have earned many awards including 4 Oscars from 12 nominations, and include *Henry V*, *Peter's Friends*, *Much Ado About Nothing*, *The Madness of King George*, *Twelfth Night* and *Wings of the Dove*. He continues to act as an independent film and theatre producer. Projects with David Parfitt, his colleague from Renaissance for Trademark Films, include *A Bunch of Amateurs*, *My Week with Marilyn*, *Parade's End* and *The Wipers Times*.

JASON TAYLOR - Lighting designer

Jason's previous productions for Out of Joint include *The Big Fellah* (with Lyric Hammersmith) and *Top Girls* (Chichester Festival Theatre). He has lit numerous productions both in the UK and internationally including twenty seasons at the Regent's Park Open Air Theatre, London. He was nominated for a Tony Award for Best Lighting Design for *Journey's End* on Broadway. His recent credits include *The American Plan* and *Our Boys* (West End/Theatre Royal Bath), *Pygmalion* (Theatre Royal Bath/UK Tour), *Afraid of the Dark* (West End*)*, *Di and Viv and Rose* (Hampstead), *The Lyons*, *Charley's Aunt* (Menier Chocolate Factory), *Daytona* (Park Theatre/ UK tour), *Horrible Histories* (Sydney Opera House), *Third Finger Left Hand* (Trafalgar Studios), *God's Property* (Talawa), *Queen of the Nile* (Hull Truck), *Laughton, The Importance of Being Earnest, The Schoolmistress, Beauty and the Beast* (Scarborough), *The Rise and Fall of Little*

Voice (UK tour), *Evita, Love Never Dies* (Copenhagen), *Copenhagen* (Sheffield). Jason has designed for many London theatres and worked at most major regional theatres including Nottingham, Sheffield, Plymouth, Birmingham, Edinburgh, Southampton, Clwyd and Liverpool.

THIS MAY HURT A BIT

Stella Feehily

Acknowledgements

With thanks to Tom Morris, Sebastian Born, the National
Theatre Studio, Laura Collier, Colin Ludlow, Lord Kinnock,
Nick Hern, Jacky Davis, Louise Irvine, Dr Lucy Reynolds,
Nicholas Timmins, Roy Lilley, Lucy Briers, Nigel Cooke,
Lorna Brown, Susan Engel, David Rintoul, Julian Wadham,
Karina Fernandez, Matthew Needham, Niamh Cusack, Ian and
Kay Redford, Dr Polly Brown, Out of Joint, Mel Kenyon,
Nigel Stafford-Clark, Bolton Octagon, Dr Bob Gill, Allyson
Pollock, Nina Steiger, Tim Hoare, Kara Manning, Sally
McKenna, Sarah Liisa Wilkinson and last but very definitely
not least Max Stafford-Clark.

This May Hurt A Bit was developed in association with the
National Theatre Studio and Out of Joint.

The books and materials that I referred to when researching the play
were: Hansard February 9th 1948; Hansard April 23rd 1951; *In Place
of Fear* by Aneurin Bevan; Pollock A, Price D and Harding-Edgar L
(2013) Briefing paper – the NHS reinstatement bill open democracy,
January, www.opendemocracy.net/ournhs/allyson-pollock-david-price-
louisa-harding-edgar/briefing-paper-nhs-reinstatement-bill;
www.socialinvestigations.blog-spot.it/2012/02/nhs-privatisation-
compilation-of.html; Foundation Trust News Report 2013; *Never
Again?* by Nicholas Timmins; *NHS SOS* by Jacky Davis and Raymond
Tallis; *The Plot Against The NHS* by Colin Leys and Stewart Player;
Dr Lucy Reynolds talks to Jill Mountford (BMJ website); *NHS PLC*
by Allyson Pollock

Special thanks to Frank and Elizabeth Brenan

S.F.

For Jacky Davis, Louise Irvine, Lucy Reynolds
And all those fighting to protect our National Health Service

4

Characters

ANEURIN BEVAN
PRIME MINISTER
MILES, *senior civil servant*
NICHOLAS JAMES
MR WEAVER, *consultant urologist*
TABITHA, *receptionist, auxiliary nurse*
DANNY, *prisoner*
SAM, *police officer*
CASSANDRA, *lady in the audience*
THE NHS
IRIS JAMES
MARIEL JAMES
DR HANK QUESTEL
WINSTON CHURCHILL
ALY, *public-health researcher*
BEA, *public-health researcher*
ROGER, *paramedic 1*
TERRY, *paramedic 2*
WENDY, *a pretty weather girl*
GINA, *nurse*
DINAH, *patient on geriatric ward*
JOHN, *stroke patient*
ARCHIE, *hospital porter*
MILTON, *a Conservative campaign strategist*
DR GRAY, *consultant*
THE GRIM REAPER

The play can be performed by a cast of eight with the following doubling of roles:

IRIS
NICHOLAS / PRIME MINISTER
ANEURIN BEVAN / DANNY / TERRY / ARCHIE
WINSTON CHURCHILL / MR WEAVER /
    ROGER / JOHN / MILTON
MARIEL / THE NHS /
TABITHA / DINAH / BEA / DR GRAY
HANK / MILES / SAM / THE GRIM REAPER
GINA / CASSANDRA / ALY / WENDY

Board of Directors to be played by all members of cast

This text went to press before the end of rehearsals and so may differ slightly from the play as performed.

Scene One

In the Beginning

ANEURIN BEVAN. Mr Speaker, I beg to move:
> That this House takes note that the appointed day for the
> National Health Service has been fixed for July 5th and
> welcomes the coming into force on that date of this measure
> which offers to all sections of the community
> comprehensive medical care and treatment and lays for the
> first time a sound foundation for the health of the people.
> The House will recollect that this debate was requested from
> this side of the House, and not by the Opposition. There is
> some significance in that fact. During the last six months to
> a year there has been a sustained propaganda in the
> newspapers supporting the Party opposite. There has been
> even worse misrepresentation, sustained by a campaign of
> personal abuse, from the BMA. From the very beginning,
> this small body of politically poisoned people have decided
> to fight the Health Act itself and to stir up as much emotion
> as they can in the profession. It has been suggested that one
> of the reasons why the medical profession are so stirred up
> is because of personal deficiencies of my own but it can
> hardly be suggested that conflict between the British
> Medical Association and the Minister of the day is a
> consequence of any deficiencies that I possess, because we
> have never been able yet to appoint a Minister of Health
> with whom the BMA agreed. My distinguished fellow
> countryman (Lloyd George) had quite a little difficulty with
> them. He was a Liberal, and they found him an anathema.
> Then there was Mr Ernest Brown who was a Liberal
> National, whatever that might mean, representing a Scottish
> constituency. They found him abominable. As for Mr
> Willink, a Conservative representing an English
> constituency, they found him intolerable. I am a Welshman,
> a Socialist representing a Welsh constituency, and they find
> me even more impossible. It is a quality which I appear to

share in common with every Minister of Health whom the British Medical Association have met.

May I say this in conclusion? I think it is a sad reflection that this great Act, to which every Party has made its contribution should have so stormy a birth.

We ought to take pride in the fact that, despite our financial and economic anxieties, we are still able to do the most civilised thing in the world – put the welfare of the sick in front of every other consideration. I hope the House will not hesitate to tell the British Medical Association that we look forward to this Act starting on 5th July 1948, and that we expect the medical profession to take their proper part in it because there is nothing in it that any doctor should be otherwise than proud to acknowledge. Let us safeguard and celebrate that.

Scene Two

March 2011. The Health and Social Care Bill is in Trouble

No. 10.

The PRIME MINISTER *and* MILES, *a senior civil servant. The* PM *is looking through the Health and Social Care Bill.*

PM. Fuck.
  (*Continues to leaf through.*)
  How many pages this time?

MILES. Three hundred and fifty-four, Prime Minister.

PM. Have you read this draft?

MILES. Yes, Prime Minister. And the previous draft – four hundred and sixty-seven pages.

PM. That's an improvement then. So what's wrong with it?

MILES. Prime Minister, what's right with it?

PM. Danny and Oliver were supposed to redraft it.

MILES. They certainly redrafted the White Paper. To be fair to Mr Alexander with his work on the deficit spending review and with the unexpected departure of Mr Laws – he has been treble jobbing – in any case neither of them are health-policy experts.

PM. Oliver promised to bomb-proof it.

MILES. Prime Minister, Oliver is Oliver.

PM. Andrew seemed to have all the answers.

MILES. But was he asked the right questions? For example – What is the narrative behind a massive reorganisation of the Health Service when it faces the biggest financial challenge in its history?
A reorganisation of this size will cost two if not three billion pounds, Prime Minister.

PM. Your lot have kept very quiet until now.

MILES. Prime Minister, it's not been easy to communicate our reservations since you got rid of the Strategy Unit.

PM. God, this row is becoming ghastly.

MILES. Yes, sir. It's very messy.
The British Medical Association, the Royal College of General Practitioners, the Royal College of Nursing, the Royal College of Midwives, the Royal College of Pathologists, the Royal College of Radiologists, the Royal College of Psychiatrists, the Royal College of Ophthalmologists, the Chartered Society of Physiotherapy, the Faculty of Public Health, the College of Occupational Therapists, the College of Emergency Medicine, Unison, Unite –
All against you – and there's the public of course.

PM. But we'll outfox the lot of them in the same way that Aneurin Bevan and Atlee did when they introduced the NHS.

MILES. Prime Minister, they had an electoral mandate...

PM. There can be no retreat, Miles –
Especially now that the Lib Dems are on side.

MILES. Indeed, Prime Minister.

PM. I could say that I hadn't read the draft bill –
That I wasn't entirely aware of extent of the reforms.
No I couldn't.
Could I?

MILES. You have that option.
If you'll just take a look. (*Opens the* PM*'s copy of the bill.*)
As you requested, I have highlighted the items that are
causing the most overwhelming opposition. These are the
sections you'll be required to answer questions on.

PM. You've highlighted almost every page.

MILES. It would appear so.
As you are aware – this revolutionary reorganisation of the
NHS is in fact an evolution of New Labour policy.

PM. We don't mention those twats.

MILES. But you should mention them and often. After all,
you're pushing through much of their unfinished business –
albeit at speed. Keep reminding them of that – and they'll
find it harder to oppose the bill.

PM. Right.

MILES. So as you know, the bill abolishes PCTs and with that –
Strategic Health Authorities, removing two tiers of
management which is a reorganisation of gigantic
proportions, giving the lie to your *No Top Down* claim.

PM. But we're now saying it's a bottom-up reorganisation.
Cutting bureaucracy. Improving patient care.

MILES. Of course – (*Shows the* PM *various pages of the bill
during the following.*)
Building on the Foundation Trust process started by the last
Government –

PM. Twats.

MILES. Indeed – all hospitals have to attain Foundation status
by 2014 – this is to encourage innovation by granting more
autonomy. Struggling hospitals will exit the market.

PM. That is – be allowed to fail?

MILES. Yes, sir, or face being taken over.
The treasury will hand over eighty billion pounds of taxpayers' money to GPs by 2013 whether the GPs are ready or not. The GPs will be involved in commissioning consortia, however there's not a shred of evidence to suggest they have the skills for commissioning health care – many of them don't even want the responsibility. It's a gamble, Prime Minister.

PM. Whose side are you on, Miles?

MILES. Very funny, Prime Minister.
This section is causing a stink –
It repeals the Secretary of State's long-standing core duty to provide or secure a comprehensive Health Service.
Meaning he can no longer be held to account legally for comprehensive health care provision.

PM. Now, that is genius. We change a few words and the NHS is at arm's length.
Go on.

MILES. Very well – the most contentious element within concerns competition – see part three chapter two, in particular clause sixty-one, *Any Willing Provider* – this is to promote competition and choice – however the inclusion of AWP gives the anti-reform brigade further evidence that this Government has an agenda of privatisation.

PM. We're going to rename AWP – Any Qualified Provider.

MILES. But there's no change in substance.
The BMA are saying that increased competition is 'damaging and risky'.

PM. I'll deal with the BMA. What's the positive narrative behind the reforms? Wrap it up in five lines.
I've got to answer questions on this bastard son of Blair and Lady Thatcher in less than half an hour.

MILES. It's a very long bill, Prime Minister, very, very detailed, very complicated –

PM. Utter bollocks?

MILES. I'm afraid so, Prime Minister. Incomprehensible.
You simply can't encapsulate the main thrust in a couple of
sentences. *Entre nous* let's be clear – there is no positive
narrative behind these reforms. They certainly won't help the
NHS address its central task of making twenty billion
pounds of efficiency savings over the next four years. A large
section of the medical community smell a giant rat and not
all of them are afraid of upsetting the Department of Health.

PM. I fucking hate PMQs.

MILES. How's this, Prime Minister – if we tackle the problems
of today we avoid a crisis tomorrow.
The Health and Social Care Bill puts clinicians at the centre
of commissioning, frees up providers to innovate –
empowers patients, and gives focus to public health.

PM. Good.
But let me make it absolutely clear – for the health of our
beloved National Health Service – we can't afford *not* to
make these changes. Or something like that?

MILES. Excellent, Prime Minister.
And if you'll give me a moment I'll find a wodge of statistics
– always helpful.

PM. I'll bring out the 'Ageing population – a drain on our NHS'
line. Always works a treat.

MILES. Blame the elderly. Very good, Prime Minister.

PM. I need a put-down.
I'll tell Ed to get some ideas of his own and stop spouting the
BMA press release.

MILES. Charming.

PM. Good. Yes. I think that's it, Miles. Easy after all.

MILES. Well, Prime Minister, you can put lipstick on a pig –
but it's still a pig.

Scene Three

2014

The Harrington Hospital. Urology Department.

MR WEAVER – *senior urology consultant – is examining* NICHOLAS*'s prostate. After some moments.*

MR WEAVER. Waiting long, Mr James?

NICHOLAS. Yes.

MR WEAVER. Angry? Hmm?

NICHOLAS. I have a pressing engagement.

MR WEAVER. Mm?

NICHOLAS. My sister is visiting from New York.

MR WEAVER. Well, I don't expect mercy.
No one knows what goes on behind these doors. Going the extra mile and all that. Last poor chap spent ten minutes crying.

NICHOLAS *makes a noise.*

I won't be a moment, Mr James.

NICHOLAS. Thank you.

MR WEAVER. Hmm hmm.

NICHOLAS. Yes?

MR WEAVER. Pop your trousers back on, Mr James, and have a seat.

MR WEAVER *whips off his rubber gloves and washes his hands.* NICHOLAS *gathers his belongings and sits by* MR WEAVER. *He puts his newspaper on the table.*

You've been referred by the Holloway Health Centre because you have a rising PSA level.

NICHOLAS. Yes. Dr McNulty is my GP there.

MR WEAVER. Is he still going?
And you did a blood test.

NICHOLAS. Last week.

MR WEAVER. Retired?

NICHOLAS. Made redundant. I've been quite depressed about it.

MR WEAVER. Taking something?

NICHOLAS. Nothing.
Vodka.

MR WEAVER. Jolly good. So looking at your blood tests. McNulty should have sent you sooner – but I expect he's under pressure to keep a lid on referrals.

NICHOLAS. Perhaps it's a form of population control.

MR WEAVER. Your PSA has been a high for a time – but the recent result has gone up significantly.

NICHOLAS. Should I be worried?

MR WEAVER (*swings around to look at* NICHOLAS). We're certainly going to have to do something about it.
(*Spots* NICHOLAS*'s newspaper.*)
Guardian reader are you? Probably still banging on about weapons of mass destruction?

NICHOLAS. When was the last time you read the *Guardian*?

MR WEAVER. Never. I suppose you believe there weren't any.

NICHOLAS. Yes I do.

MR WEAVER. Of course there were. You just have to look in the order book. Nobody can find that now can they! Ha, ha, ha, ha. A ruddy great 'Made in Wiltshire' on the damn things. (*Buzzes to the nurse outside.*) Tabitha, we're out of Prostap injections.

NICHOLAS. Injection?

TABITHA. On the way, Mr Weaver.

MR WEAVER. We just don't know the half of it. I meet a lot of top politicians for the waterworks. They all go private of course – ha, ha, ha. Pop your trousers down please, Mr James, and hop back up on the bed.

NICHOLAS. They're making billions in cuts and seeing you privately? (*Unbuckles his trousers again.*)

MR WEAVER. I know. Absolute bloody chaos.

NICHOLAS *starts to take off his trousers.*

Not off completely – we've done that one. It's your stomach I want. Where is that girl? (*Buzzes to reception.*) Tabitha? TABITHA.

TABITHA. Sorry, Mr Weaver. Is it the one in the blue box?

MR WEAVER. Yes. Yes. Come along, Tabitha.

NICHOLAS. Next time you treat a 'top politician' tell them to cut Trident and they'll fund all the hospitals in the country.

MR WEAVER. China delivered some pretty clever rockets to Iran. Your *Guardian* didn't tell you that did it? Rockets are pointing in this direction. Do you want an A and E department or protection on these shores?

TABITHA *enters with a blue box. She takes out a syringe from it.*

TABITHA. Sorry, Mr Weaver. I got waylaid.

MR WEAVER. Thank you, Tabitha – but I should have a supply of them.
I feel like I'm talking to the wall. Bring me a handful of VT leaflets.

TABITHA (*fighting back tears*). Yes, Mr Weaver. Sorry. I'll get on to it straight away.

NICHOLAS. What will the injection do?

MR WEAVER. With any luck it should bring your PSA level down – by stopping the production of testosterone that is. We want to reduce your prostate, which frankly is the size of a space hopper. However it will hit you in the libido.

NICHOLAS. I'll be unable to get an erection?

MR WEAVER *checks the syringe and prepares the site of injection with a swab.*

MR WEAVER. You'll have about as much chance as a snowstorm in August.

MR WEAVER *places the syringe at* NICHOLAS*'s stomach.*

Now –
Concern about the loss of manhood or the role of sexual intimacy can cause a great deal of distress. Though we should be realistic – dysfunction is treatable.

NICHOLAS. I'm not bothered about that. I'm a widower.

TABITHA *enters with the leaflet.*

TABITHA. It's the vacuum therapy leaflet? Blue also.

MR WEAVER (*irritably*). Yes, yes. Thank you, Tabitha.

TABITHA *exits.*

How does it work? Lightweight compact device. Pump, pump, pump for a couple of minutes. Pulls in blood *et voilà*. Fully ready to go. It's got a super-quiet battery. Four size types. You can use it as often as you like and let me tell you – it really does work. There's the address for private orders – they are not available on the NHS any more. Now whatever you do – don't use a vacuum cleaner instead. It's an awkward trip to A and E with a household appliance stuck to your Percy.

NICHOLAS. Do I have prostate cancer?

MR WEAVER. It's possible.

A knock at the door.

(*To the knock.*) Yes?

TABITHA. Oh sorry, Mr Weaver. We got eight medical students to observe?

MR WEAVER. That's fine isn't it? (*To the students.*) Come in. Don't stand there hovering at the door.

NICHOLAS. I didn't think –

MR WEAVER. Probably got another ten – maybe even fifteen years in you.

NICHOLAS. Really? Ten years? Please ask them to wait.

MR WEAVER. What do you expect, man? To live for ever?
We'll get you back in three months and see how you are.
Here's my card if you want to see me privately then it can be
as soon as you like.

MR WEAVER *places the syringe at* NICHOLAS's *stomach*.

What's the expression?
British patients would rather not die and be immortal.
American patients think they are immortal.

NICHOLAS. I have this sudden feeling like it's all over.

MR WEAVER. Yes, it's depressing isn't it. Okay, Mr James,
this may hurt a bit.

Scene Four

Harrington Health NHS Trust. We Care About Your Views

Urology Outpatients waiting area.

*Yellow walls. A grey dado rail. Posters reminding people to
wash their hands, one advertises a talk on Prostate Cancer
Management, one stating 'Harrington Health NHS Trust. We
Care About Your Views' hangs askew on the wall.*

A table of tatty magazines, ES *supplements, car magazines,
couple of* Metros. *A plastic jug of water and some plastic cups.*

TABITHA, *a truculent auxiliary nurse/receptionist, is chatting
on the phone.*

DANNY, *a prisoner, is in the waiting area and is handcuffed to*
SAM, *a police officer.*

TABITHA (*on the phone*). Babes, I keep telling them I don't get
overtime –
No one listens to me.

I know. Exactly. Why can't fat bitch drag the bags? But they
say Fatima has a bad back so I have to do it. Boo hoo.
Tough shit.
(*To the waiting patients*.) Mr Mohammed Al Hussaini?
Room one.
Mr Al Hussaini?

NICHOLAS *approaches the appointments desk. He hands*
TABITHA *an appointment follow-up from* MR WEAVER.

DANNY. Lady! It's an abuse of power making people wait.

SAM. Shush.

TABITHA (*to* NICHOLAS). Take a seat.

TABITHA *turns away from* NICHOLAS *and continues her
conversation.*

And, babes, Weaver has been shouting all morning.
All morning.
I'll walk if he –
Are you at home?

NICHOLAS. When you have quite finished your conversation –
I'd like to make a three-month check-up appointment with
Mr Weaver.

TABITHA. Take a seat for me.

NICHOLAS. I don't want to take a seat for you.

TABITHA *opens her mouth in outrage and tuts.*

TABITHA. Call you back, babes.

She hangs up and checks the computer.

Oh. (*Types again*.) What is that?
I'm afraid I can't access your details.

MR WEAVER *buzzes.*

Yes, Mr Weaver.

Mr Yakubu Ikoku. Room three.

NICHOLAS. Mr Weaver was looking at them only moments
ago.

TABITHA. Yeah, but they're not available now.

NICHOLAS. Are they lost? Misplaced?

TABITHA. The hospital has looked for your details.
And can't access them. So I am unable to make that further
appointment – at the moment – sir.

NICHOLAS. That seems very silly. Who is the hospital?

TABITHA. I don't understand.

NICHOLAS. You said the hospital has looked for my details.
Who is the hospital?

TABITHA. Please don't shout at me. (*Points to a sign, which
says 'Abuse of NHS Staff Will Not Be Tolerated'.*) As part of
our application to become a Foundation Trust – a private
business so to speak – we're going 'paperless' to improve
efficiency.

NICHOLAS. Sorry?

TABITHA. Digitisation.

NICHOLAS. So?

TABITHA. I'm now going to have to call India.

NICHOLAS. For what?

TABITHA. Technical support.

NICHOLAS. Bloody hell. Just write down my details.

TABITHA. Don't shout at me.

NICHOLAS. I'm not shouting at you.

TABITHA. It's not my fault. It's the computer.
We're under a lot of pressure, sir.

NICHOLAS. I don't understand why you can't just write my
details down?

TABITHA *bursts into tears*.

TABITHA. What good would that do?

NICHOLAS. Okay. Okay. I'll wait. I'll wait.

TABITHA. Take a seat. I'll call you when I resolve the
technical issue.
Mrs Soraya Perez? Room two. Mrs Perez?

NICHOLAS. Sorry. I didn't mean to upset you. (*Sits down.*)

TABITHA *makes a phone call.*

DANNY. Don't be. You've got to push and push or they walk
all over you. You wait and wait for your appointment and
then there's always hassle. Rude as fuck.

TABITHA. Tabitha!

SAM. The way things are structured – it does seem a failure of
imagination.

TABITHA. Yeah, I've lost thousands of records.

DANNY. They don't understand us. None of them are British.

NICHOLAS. That young lady is from London.
South at a guess.

DANNY. Next she'll be saying she's 'just obeying orders'.

TABITHA. Yeah, I'm doing that.

DANNY *groans loudly.*

Sir?

DANNY. Is there a doctor in the house?

SAM. He's fine. Sorry, miss.

DANNY. It's a disgrace and reception has all the charm of the
politburo.
This used to be a great hospital.

TABITHA. Just turn it off and on? Right.

DANNY. You in for waterworks?

NICHOLAS. Sort of. You?

SAM. Aggravated burglary.

DANNY. It's my bladder.
Think they're going to whip it out.

NICHOLAS. Sorry about that.

DANNY. Gonna have a bag.
    Just for pee.

SAM. It's called a stoma.
    He smokes too much.

DANNY. Is my ex-wife in the room?

SAM. It's directly linked to bladder cancer.

DANNY. Need a fag right now to be honest.
    Bloody hell. Ninety minutes I've been waiting. Ninety
    minutes eh?
    They don't give a nun's knickers.
    Anyway – I don't care if I live or die.

SAM. You'll have me crying next.

DANNY. You'll miss me. You see.

SAM. Maggie will miss you.

DANNY. I love Maggie. That's true.
    (*To* NICHOLAS.) Ex-wife has got custody.

NICHOLAS. Are you able to – call her? Maggie?
    Where you are I mean?

DANNY. She's a budgie.

NICHOLAS. Ah.

SAM. Got a new joke for you.

DANNY. He's about as funny as cancer.

SAM. Why wouldn't the stoma bag stay on?

DANNY. Just get on with it.

SAM. Because it was pissed off.

DANNY. Terrible, pal. Terrible.
    Ladies and gentlemen – the brightest and best of the
    Metropolitan Police.

CASSANDRA (*from audience*). Excuse me? Yes? You?

NICHOLAS. Hello?

He gets up and moves towards CASSANDRA.

CASSANDRA. You've got it all wrong. It's not that they don't give a nun's knickers – it's that the hospital is being starved of funds.
The plan is to let it fail so it can be taken over by the private sector.
Why doesn't anybody understand this?

TABITHA. Do you mind? I'm working here.
Could someone get front of house?

CASSANDRA. Following the Health and Social Care Bill in 2013 the Government passed regulations locking privatisation into health care provision in England.

DANNY (*to* SAM). Why don't you do something? Arrest her.

SAM. I'm a bit busy.

CASSANDRA. It's part of a power grab by US companies – a trade treaty which will enable them to take over our public services.
We're facing the possibility of irreversible privatisation – in only a few years.

SAM. Come along now, miss. We don't want any trouble.

CASSANDRA. The Health Service has been restructured onto an insurance-compatible footing in order to harmonise it with the US system.

STAGE MANAGEMENT *enter the auditorium and attempt to remove her.*

SAM. You've had your fun – now move along, miss.

CASSANDRA. The NHS is not going to be privatised overnight but in five years' time it's going to look very different. We've been betrayed. We've got to do something. Tell your family, friends, colleagues, the person beside you – you could die because services are going to deteriorate.

CASSANDRA *is removed from the auditorium.*

TABITHA. Mr Richards? Mr Richards! Mr Solanji will see you now.

SAM. Right, Daniel. Come on then, son.

DANNY. Nice to talk to you, pal.
You meet a better class of person in Urology outpatients.

SAM. Hope you get sorted. Be lucky.

SAM *nods a goodbye at* NICHOLAS *and exits with* DANNY.

NICHOLAS *gets up – stands before* TABITHA *who is looking at her computer.*

NICHOLAS. How are we doing?

TABITHA. Okay, Mr James. September 29th suit?

NICHOLAS. But that's over five months away. I need an appointment in three.

TABITHA. It's all we have available, sir.
Will I make that September 29th appointment for you?

An ambulance siren. A paramedic pushing a gurney forward disturbs the scene.

SAM *gets up to join this scene.*

Scene Five

The NHS is Unwell

A siren. ROGER *(paramedic 1) is in the process of hooking a frail woman up to an IV machine.* SAM *the police officer interviews him.*

ROGER. This is a sixty-five-year-old lady. She is very dehydrated, very confused.
She's fallen a few times. Very poorly indeed. We believe she's been without food, water and medication for the best part of a week. She's been using her front room as a convenience. Up until last week she had been cared for by an agency contracted by the council but those services have been taken over by private company *Compassionate Care Agency* –

SAM. Say no more.

ROGER. Somehow the lady's details were removed from the register. The alarm was raised by concerned neighbours. I see this kind of thing all the time.

SAM. That's life though, isn't it. (*Writing.*) Without the provision of food, water or medication.

ROGER. That is correct.

SAM. So is she whack-a-doodle gaga?

ROGER. We believe she's half-a-doodle gaga.

SAM. Any family?

ROGER. Not living.

SAM. Who'd be old, eh? I'd rather have a coronary than Alzheimer's. I'd rather a massive stroke than to live a semi-life like this. I'm upping my butter, cream, red meat, booze. Going back on the fags. No more *five-a-day* for me. I'd rather a good life and a quick death. Bang, I'm gone. None of this dying-embers-of-my life business, smelling of piss, not knowing my wife, my daughters, not caring if I've shaved or crapped my pants. Dependent? Can't do it. Shoot me. Right. She's all yours.

He exits.

ROGER. All right, young lady? Feeling a bit better? I'll see if I can rustle up a doctor.

The woman sits up – she is THE NHS.

THE NHS. Clem was the one. The best. It was such a hopeful relationship, so full of promise. Took us a quite a time to get together. Beveridge introduced us.
Such an awful lot of talk and strife before but by jingo, 1948 was a year to remember. Of course, it wasn't to last and then I had a succession of rather indifferent liaisons, Winston, Anthony, Harold, Alec, then Harold – the little man from Huddersfield, Edward – well. I suppose you could say at least Edward was committed to me, then got back with Huddersfield Harold, he lacked conviction but he really was rather decent, and poor old Jim, so hamstrung. None of them could top that first spark of pure energy. None of them knew what to do with me. Some resented me – for sure, but nobody tried to ruin me – until Margaret, with whom I found myself in a long painful relationship. She cut me to the bone. Quite dangerous – in the end, like them all, she got the boot but her legacy lingers. I'll skip over John, Tony was the most tremendous disappointment – he fell in love with city boys – but in the beginning I thought he was really something, Gordon was – well, he was just so angry, wasn't he? But the current one? He thinks he's a lover – with his constant declarations. I love you, I love you, now Change!
He says I must heal myself –
So why won't he let me alone?
What a shit.

Scene Six

Is This the Britain We Fought the War For?

Lunch with the James family.

IRIS *is holding up a painting.*

IRIS. But what is it?

MARIEL. That's the wrong way up. If you hold it the other way, Mummy!

IRIS. Ah, now I see.
Despite the fact my grandson paints in the style of Vermeer, I still have no idea what to do with a picture of the male genitalia. Couldn't he paint a tree or something?

MARIEL. Mother – my son is not attending New York's finest art school so he can paint a tree.

NICHOLAS. Very liberal of you, Mariel.

MARIEL. First dig of the day. Noted.
Mum, Tom was so excited for you to have it. It's his gift to you.

IRIS. Oh dear. Is it?
My new cleaner, Reina, is refusing to dust his painting of 'The Hairy Pomegranates'. I'm not sure I can put her through this.

MARIEL. Mummy, a cleaner is a cleaner.

NICHOLAS. How was your flight, Hank?

HANK. Nicholas, I resent the hours trapped in a titanium tube. Really disturbs my system.

MARIEL. I was medicated so we probably won't stay too long, Mummy.
I might keel over after this glass of wine.

MARIEL *takes* IRIS*'s hand.*

IRIS. Ditto.

NICHOLAS. Where are you staying in London, Mariel?

MARIEL. The Dorchester – where the conference is being held.

HANK. I'm giving a paper on Arthroplasty and Glenoid
Reconstruction.
It's the Bone and Joint Decade World Network Conference.

IRIS. There's a day you won't get back again.

HANK. I am looking forward to it, Iris.

MARIEL. He's a wonderful speaker.

HANK. Oh darling.

MARIEL. You are. You are wonderful.
Nicholas, before you arrived, I was telling Mummy that
we've moved from Manhattan to Peekskill.

HANK. We've got a beautiful condo overlooking the Hudson
River.

NICHOLAS. You must be doing awfully well.

MARIEL. Hank was made head of department at the New York
Presbyterian Hotel of Columbia Cornell.

NICHOLAS. You mean hospital surely?

MARIEL. Did I say hotel?
The New York Presbyterian has rather a grand lobby like the
Four Seasons in Mexico City.

NICHOLAS. I'm not conversant with such glamour.

HANK. You should be. Nicholas, you should visit us. Now that
you have a little more time on your hands.

NICHOLAS. What?

MARIEL. Mummy told us that you were made redundant...
we know.

HANK. That's rough. Sorry to hear it, Nick.

IRIS. It happened when the school got a new head, a slashed
budget, and a decimated art department. They kept the two
young teachers.

HANK. Cheaper that way no doubt.

MARIEL. Can they do that? Are you going to sue?

NICHOLAS. I'm of retirement age.

IRIS. He was there for twelve years.
Outrageous. Been terribly upset about it.

HANK. Perhaps it's a good time to take things easy? Enjoy
your life.

NICHOLAS. Hank, my wife died two years ago.

HANK. Yes. Of course. Lovely Anna. You need to take your
mind off things.
I understand.

NICHOLAS. Besides – I don't want to retire. I don't feel old.

MARIEL. But it won't be easy to find a new teaching post at
sixty-six.
Who is going to want you?
You should take up a hobby. You used to run marathons in
the old days.

NICHOLAS. Too old to qualify as a MAMIL.

HANK. What's that?

NICHOLAS. Middle-Aged Man In Lycra.

HANK. Consult your cardiologist first. I've seen too many
fatalities when old men suddenly re-engage with physical
activity.

IRIS. Didn't you have a hospital appointment this morning?

NICHOLAS. Mm.

IRIS. Urology. Is that what you said? How did that go?

HANK. Prostate? We're all at that age.
What did your consultant have to say?

NICHOLAS. He was pushing some sort of injection.

HANK. Probably an antiandrogen. Stops testosterone.
Shrinks the balls.

MARIEL. Isn't that what they give to paedophiles?

HANK. Watch out for the mood swings.

NICHOLAS. What mood swings?

HANK. The consultant has given you the menopause by
    injection.
    So hot flushes, night sweats, breasts. And rage to look
    forward to.

MARIEL. An impotent rage. How unfair. Sorry, I shouldn't
    laugh.

NICHOLAS. He mentioned nothing of the sort but he was
    rather brusque.

HANK. A National Health Service consultant. Hmm...

MARIEL. There are many things I could say about the NHS –

HANK. You get what you pay for.

NICHOLAS. I've paid a lot of tax over forty-five years.

IRIS. I won't hear a word against it. I had wonderful treatment
    at the Harrington last year.

HANK. Speaking as a disgusting American capitalist – and
    orthopaedic surgeon – our system works so much better
    than yours.
    No queues. No waiting lists.

NICHOLAS. We know all about your system, Hank, and we
    don't want it.

HANK. When there's a bottom line – shit gets done.

NICHOLAS. 'Shit' costs, Hank.

IRIS. Some of us are eating.

HANK. Sure – the insurance system can be problematic.
    But it's not remotely as screwed up as your system.

IRIS. Hardly an endorsement of the American way, Hank.

NICHOLAS. I must invoke Colonel Thomas Rainsborough –

MARIEL. Must you?

NICHOLAS. He said – I think that the poorest he that is in
    England, hath a life to live as the greatest he.

MARIEL. Is he still doing that, Mummy?

IRIS. Stop being provocative, Mariel.

NICHOLAS. Didn't you used to be a Socialist?

MARIEL. Not for at least thirty years.

HANK. There's something deeply incoherent about political beliefs simply based on an aspiration to equality with no thought to the cost.

NICHOLAS. People go bankrupt in the US over health care. That's all I need to know.

HANK. People die waiting for treatment here. That's all I need to know.

MARIEL. Private health care should be an aspiration like owning a nice car so you can avoid the ghastly Tube.

HANK. Yes, if the wealthy used private health care, ordinary Joes would have at least have a better funded service.

IRIS. Middle-class flight would leave us with your hideous insurance system.

NICHOLAS. That's right, Mum. Social solidarity still counts for something in this country.

MARIEL. The notion that we must all be cured alongside each other for the sake of solidarity is ludicrous. What about quality? I've been reading hair-raising stories.

NICHOLAS. The *Daily Mail*?

MARIEL. My guilty online pleasure.

IRIS. It's bad for your health, Mariel.

MARIEL. But, whole hospitals have been implicated. Even with irrefutable evidence it's still impossible to criticise it.

IRIS. Bloody right. A few bad stories shouldn't damn the entire system.
And the Secretary of State for Health is constantly critical of it.
How does that help? I'm very concerned where this constant criticism will lead us.

NICHOLAS. The way of dentistry.

IRIS. The British people will never let that happen.

NICHOLAS. It's happening.

HANK. I believe the reforms are creating a better service – dare
I say, a better England.

IRIS. Bollocks, Hank.
A better England has been overwhelmed by the rush to
austerity and is buried under a toxic cloud of lobbying.

MARIEL. Mummy, really.

NICHOLAS. Strivers, skivers, the country must take the
medicine, the Health Service is broken.
Clearly the Coalition Government is waging a war of
ideology.
Our language has become so corrupted by their advertising
speak we no longer realise it. We face not just a fight for the
soul of the NHS but a fight for our souls – for England's.

MARIEL. Excuse me while I throw up.

IRIS. Mariel!

MARIEL. Wazzy old lefty hand-wringing.
Why can't we talk about *Homeland* or *Breaking Bad* like
normal families?

IRIS. Freedom from the fear of the costs of ill health. That's
what we have now. Can you imagine the time before that? Of
course you can't. Well, I can. We must never go back.

MARIEL. The war is over, Mum! Yes, the NHS is the envy of
the world –
The third world! And that's why every Somali or whoever
from Sub-Saharan Africa is desperate to get here – have their
children and whatever else they can freeload from the state.

NICHOLAS. I can't believe I am related to you.

MARIEL. Unlike you – I see the situation very clearly.
The NHS has reached the age of retirement.

IRIS. Nye Bevan once said –
Whenever you scratch a Tory you find a fascist.

MARIEL. Mummy, that's so rude.

From the audience.

WINSTON CHURCHILL. Well, Bevan would say that wouldn't he.

IRIS. Is that Sir Winston Churchill?

CHURCHILL. Yes, madam.

IRIS. Would you care for a plate of food, Sir Winston?

CHURCHILL. A delightful offer but I'd rather have a drink.

IRIS. Nicholas, take this to Sir Winston. (*Pours him a large whiskey.*)

CHURCHILL. How do you suggest we cope financially with the frail elderly, the advances in technology, the vast numbers of fat people?

IRIS. That's very cheeky of you, Sir Winston – when we created the NHS the country was literally bankrupt.

NICHOLAS. Get rid of the obsession with the market.

CHURCHILL. With all due respect, that's a bit wet.
You fear the market.
But it delivers choice and competition. This will raise standards which quite frankly is urgently needed.

IRIS. They said that privatising the railways would make them efficient and cost-effective. Would they say that now?

CHURCHILL. The Prime Minister has gone to great lengths to convince you that your NHS is safe in his hands. The collective interest is very important to him.

NICHOLAS. Since when has the market worked in the collective interest?

CHURCHILL. The Tories are a changed party.

BEVAN. Yes. They are vastly worse than before.

CHURCHILL. Bevan, you always were a squalid nuisance.

IRIS. A Scotch for Mr Bevan.

BEVAN. Don't you worry, cariad, I'll get it myself.

He walks on stage – followed by CHURCHILL.

Why is it that as the nation's health goes up the Tory spirit goes down?

CHURCHILL. I do not resent criticism, even when, for the sake of emphasis, it parts for a time with reality.

BEVAN. Because you think it spells electoral defeat.

CHURCHILL. What do you suggest we do with this financial catastrophe with which your party has burdened the country?

BEVAN. That excuse is wearing very thin. The state of the economy is the fault of an epic failure of the free market – not because the Labour Government paid too much to nurses.

CHURCHILL. It would be a great reform in politics if wisdom could be made to spread as easily and rapidly as folly.

BEVAN. Over the years I've listened to a great deal of bloated nonsense from your side of the house, but the Etonian is a bloody barefaced liar.

CHURCHILL. That's not exactly true.

BEVAN. 'No more top-down reorganisation. We will not endanger Universal Coverage. We will not lose control of waiting times,' and the biggest lie of all – 'We will not sell off the NHS.' This destruction is not only a crime against the people of England but it's a constitutional outrage.

CHURCHILL. Cameron lacks the clear principles for deliberate destruction.

BEVAN. That's as maybe – but he's still in charge of the wrecking ball.

CHURCHILL. He couldn't have done what he's done without your lot, now, could he?

HANK. Nick, who is the other guy?

NICHOLAS. That is Aneurin Bevan. Socialist. Founder of the National Health Service. Born 1897. Tredegar. Mining.

Background of poverty, self-taught, became one of the most important ministers of the post-war Labour Government. Visionary. Genius orator –

BEVAN. Bon viveur –

NICHOLAS. – Political extremist, a left-wing firebrand. One of a kind – makes the current lot look like pygmies. Died 1960.

HANK. Ah, okay. Thank you.

CHURCHILL. Across Europe, countries are cutting Health Service budgets in order to deal with the debt caused by the banking crisis.

BEVAN. This assault on the Health Service is not to do with the banking crisis but it is about money. It's about private organisations seeking to profit from public service.

IRIS. But what should we do?

BEVAN. The NHS will last as long as there are folk left with the faith to fight for it.

Scene Seven

We'd like to interrupt this scene and bring you a short message about Private Finance Initiative Schemes

ALY *and* BEA *– two public-health researchers – come forward and speak to the audience.*

ALY. Who knows what a Private Finance Initiative Scheme is?

BEA. Is it a piece of economic sorcery?

ALY. It's debt.

BEA. That debt is affecting your hospitals.

ALY. And you are paying for it.

BEA. In 1992 the Conservative Government needed money for hospitals, roads, schools, prisons – however they also wanted to cut public spending.

ALY. So – a bright spark in the treasury decided that Private Finance Initiative Schemes were just the ticket.

BEA. This involved the private sector funding and constructing new buildings – leasing them to the public sector – at very high rates of interest –

ALY. And locking the public sector into thirty- or fifty-year contracts to repay the debt.

BEA. Lovely new buildings sprang up all over 1990s Britain – what's more – the borrowing didn't appear on the balance sheets.

ALY. In 1997 New Labour thought PFIs such a great idea that they used them with complete abandon.

BEA. While in opposition, George Osborne dismissed PFIs as 'discredited'–

ALY. But in his first year as Chancellor he pressed ahead with sixty-one schemes worth a total of six point nine billion pounds.

ALLY *and* BEA *hold up a graph.*

BEA. I'd like to draw your attention to this graph. The top bump represents the private sectors eight point three billion pound outlay for public-service investment and the bottom bump represents the fifty-three billion pounds it costs the taxpayer to repay that investment –

ALY. Some PFI charges could be described as 'One hospital for the price of two' – which has forced a number of Health Trusts to sell off their buildings and land.

BEA. It's not patient demand or an ageing population that will drive NHS services to the wall but a lack of funding and crippling PFI interest repayments.

ALY. PFIs are the direct privatisation of buildings and estate we were given by our grandparents

ALY *and* BEA. Why aren't you angry?

Scene Eight

HANK *drains his glass of wine.*

HANK. The ugly capitalist has gotta use the little boy's room.

IRIS. Fire away.

MARIEL. Up the stairs. First door on the right, cookie.

> IRIS *picks up the painting and some dishes.*

> We'll do that, Mummy.

IRIS. It's all right, darling. Let me.

> IRIS *exits to the kitchen.*

> NICHOLAS *and* MARIEL *start to clear up.*

MARIEL. You should really see someone about your hostility.

NICHOLAS. I don't know what you mean.

MARIEL. Proselytising about the NHS, railing against the Tories. You haven't moved on politically in thirty years. Grow up, big brother.

NICHOLAS. Little sis, your head is so far up your –

MARIEL. You are not going to rattle me today. My analyst said I mustn't let you and I won't.

IRIS. Behave, you two.

NICHOLAS (*to* IRIS). Sorry, Mum.
(*To* MARIEL.) Let's just stop talking.

MARIEL. Fine with me.

> *They continue to clear up in silence.*

> How's Mummy?

NICHOLAS. She's in good form don't you think?

MARIEL. She looks well but she's really quite unsteady on her feet.
We should organise a carer for her.

NICHOLAS. She doesn't want one. Mariel, she doesn't want one.

MARIEL. That's not the point. I know she fell last year and
hurt her hip.
She mentioned it to Hank in passing. Hadn't remembered
that we didn't know. Thanks a bunch for telling me.

NICHOLAS. She didn't want you to know.

MARIEL. She's my mother. You should tell me

NICHOLAS. You don't live in this country.

IRIS *re-enters*.

IRIS. Don't talk about me behind my back.

MARIEL. I was saying that we should organise a carer for you.

IRIS. Don't fuss, Mariel, for goodness' sake.
I get along perfectly well by myself when you're not here.

MARIEL. We could do more for you. Don't you think, Nick?

IRIS. Nick does everything I need. Where is Hank?

NICHOLAS. Yes, what's he doing up there? Checking what
Toilet Duck we use?

MARIEL. He's had kind of a loose bowel.
Air travel does it to him.

NICHOLAS. Great. Just great.
Why doesn't he bring his loose bowel to your suite at
The Dorchester?

MARIEL. You're terribly unfunny.

IRIS. Will you two stop bickering, for heaven's sake?

NICHOLAS. Mum, Hank turned my beautiful sister into a
Republican.
Is there anything we can give her for it?

MARIEL. You're being an asshole.

IRIS. That's enough.

NICHOLAS. In England we say arsehole.

IRIS. Enough.

HANK *returns*.

HANK. Honey, I'm afraid jet lag is kicking into to this old bear.

MARIEL. I'm ready to go now.

IRIS. Oh dear. So soon, darling? Well, if you must.

MARIEL. We'll drop by after the conference tomorrow.

IRIS. Lovely. I can't wait to hear how Hank's Glenoid Reconstruction paper is received.

HANK. Thanks for a wonderful afternoon, Iris. I so enjoy these get-togethers.

IRIS. At least you do, Hank.

HANK. Catch you tomorrow, Nicholas.

MARIEL. Will you be here tomorrow?

NICHOLAS. Probably.

MARIEL *and* NICHOLAS *kiss each other on each cheek.*

MARIEL. Fuck pig.

NICHOLAS. Witch hag.

MARIEL. Bye, Mummy.

IRIS. Bye, darling.

NICHOLAS *follows them out.*

IRIS *picks up some letters and papers and starts to read.*

NICHOLAS *re-enters.*

NICHOLAS. God.

IRIS. You shouldn't fight with Mariel like that. We only see them once a year.

NICHOLAS. Sorry, Mum.

IRIS. She can be a frightful pain and Hank is an insufferable bore but I had rather hoped you two had grown out of that sort of thing.

NICHOLAS. I shouldn't row with her – you're absolutely right.

IRIS. I dug out these letters your father wrote before we were married. I wanted to show them to you and Mariel but you were both being so obstreperous I couldn't bear it.

NICHOLAS. Oh dear. I am sorry about that. Tomorrow then? I promise I won't provoke Mariel no matter what she says.

IRIS. Yes and pigs might fly.

NICHOLAS. May I see?

IRIS *passes him a letter and he reads.*

'I do not believe a war will come for several years yet but by God when it does – those of us who are not killed – must urge change. England must become a better, fairer country – or else it won't be worth the sacrifice. A cheerful conclusion to a letter written to express my heartfelt wishes for your happiness. Yours sincerely, Charles James.'
Is that supposed to be a love letter from Daddy?

IRIS. Read on.

NICHOLAS. 'PS – In the midst of all this uncertainty – I feel impelled to propose marriage. As soon as you are eighteen I will come down to Pembroke and go to your father directly.'
Did my father spot you in your school uniform?
The dirty devil.

IRIS. He did. He did. We met on a train. I was captain of tennis – We were coming back from an away match at Penrhos College.
Read on.

NICHOLAS. '*PPS* – Please stop kissing Freddie Blanchard. He is an idiot.'

IRIS *starts to cry.*

IRIS. Poor Freddie was killed at Monte Cassino. Still makes me sad.
He only had to hold on for another few months and the war would have been over.

NICHOLAS. Don't cry, Mum. You'll make me cry.

He comforts her.

IRIS. I hope you're happy, Nicholas. I know your sister is happy. She's oblivious really. I know how you must miss Anna but well, I won't be around for many more years.

NICHOLAS. Don't say that.

IRIS. You must live, live! You're only a boy really.

NICHOLAS. Don't you worry about me, Mum.

IRIS. I'll lie down for a bit.
Just let yourself out.
I'm going to get into bed with Carlos the Jackal.

NICHOLAS. What?

IRIS *slowly makes her way out.*

IRIS. Reina lent me the DVD. Horrifically violent I fear.

NICHOLAS *tries to lend an arm to assist.*

No, no. I'm perfectly all right.

NICHOLAS. I'll just finish tidying up here.
I'll come over tomorrow morning with your shopping.

IRIS. And to see Hank and Mariel.

NICHOLAS. Of course.

IRIS. Put the dishwasher on.

NICHOLAS *does so and then picks up the letters to read.*

There is a sound of a crash.

Silence.

NICHOLAS. Mother?

He runs out.

Scene Nine

One hour later.

IRIS *is lying on the couch. Ambulance siren.* NICHOLAS *enters followed by two* PARAMEDICS.

ROGER. Oh hello. Right. Good afternoon.

NICHOLAS. We've been waiting an hour.

TERRY. We come when we get the call, sir.

NICHOLAS. Unbelievable.

ROGER *kneels down beside* IRIS *and takes her hand.*

ROGER. Hello, dear.

IRIS. Who are you?

ROGER. My name is Roger. I work for the ambulance service.

IRIS. Where's Charles?

NICHOLAS. Daddy died twenty years ago.

IRIS. Good God. No one told me?

TERRY. Can you tell me what's happened, sir?

IRIS. Who are you?

ROGER. My name is Roger. I work for the ambulance service, darlin'.

NICHOLAS. She's had a fall. She's very confused.

ROGER. How are you feeling, darlin'?

IRIS. I'm very well, thank you. (*Looks around.*) This is a nice house.

NICHOLAS. You live here.

IRIS. Goody.

TERRY. What's her name?

NICHOLAS. Mrs Iris James.

TERRY. Is she on any medication?

NICHOLAS. Blood pressure.

IRIS. What's all this?

ROGER. Take a BP, Terry. Sorry to barge in on you like this, darlin'. Is this her normal level of response?

NICHOLAS. No. She's normally in the whole of her mind and health.

ROGER. Did she hit her head?

NICHOLAS. She may have.

ROGER. Iris? Hello, dear.

TERRY. You've had a bit of a fall, Mrs James.

ROGER. Bradycardic, Terry.

TERRY. Mrs James? Do you have any pain?

IRIS. No. Who are you?

TERRY. I'm Terry, darlin'. I work for the ambulance service. 186 over 90, Roge.
I'm just going to have a quick look to see if you hurt yourself.

IRIS. Where's Charles?

NICHOLAS. Oh, Mum.

IRIS. What are you doing?

ROGER. That's it. Well done.

TERRY. No broken bones, Roge.

ROGER. It's all right. Can you lift your arms, Iris?

IRIS. I can.

NICHOLAS. Is it a stroke?

TERRY. Her face hasn't dropped. She has speech.
She's not paralysed – Could be a transient ischaemic attack.

ROGER. Could you lift them then, darlin'?

IRIS. Lift what?

TERRY. Your arms?

IRIS. Why would I do that?
   Who are you?

TERRY. My name is Terry and I work for the ambulance service.

IRIS. This is a nice house.

NICHOLAS. Why is she repeating herself?

ROGER. We're not sure at the moment.
   Terry, do a blood glucose.

IRIS. I want to go to the bathroom.
   Blast the wretches.

ROGER. Settle down, my darlin'. What day is it today?

IRIS. I don't know.

TERRY. Five point four.

ROGER. When were you born?

IRIS. Impertinent.

TERRY. Who is the current Prime Minister?

IRIS. That's a very silly question.
   Ted Heath of course.

ROGER. She's not joking is she.

NICHOLAS. No.

IRIS. What are they doing here?

ROGER. Mrs James, we're going to have to take you to A and E.

NICHOLAS. Take her to the Harrington. It's her local hospital.

IRIS. Oh fuck.
   Hospitals kill.

ROGER. Her heart rate is slow. Blood pressure high, Terry.
   We'll do an ECG in the ambulance.

IRIS. What am I doing here? I'm dizzy, Nicholas.

NICHOLAS. It's been an hour already. Please take us to the
   Harrington.

TERRY. Yes, sir. All right, young lady. We're going to have to move you.

The PARAMEDICS *help* IRIS *into a wheelchair.*

Can you get her medication, sir?

NICHOLAS. Everything is going to be all right.

NICHOLAS *exits.*

TERRY. Okay, sweetheart. That's it.

They turn to face the audience.

ROGER. Governments never learn the lesson of former administrations that changing structures in the NHS doesn't work. They all think it's a matter of simply legislating and then hey presto – a wonderful working system will appear and it will all be lovely.

TERRY. All of us working for the NHS know that reorganisation is a diversion not a solution – this matters little to the politicians who simply live within an election cycle.

ROGER. We all need to pull together now.

NICHOLAS *re-enters.*

IRIS. Blast the wretches. Charles, Charles?

NICHOLAS. She's calling for my father.
Is this it? Is this how it goes?

ROGER. We're going to make sure she is well taken care of. And now it's over to Wendy at the Weather Centre.

TERRY. Any good news for us, Wendy?

Scene Ten

A map of hospital closures and hospitals under threat of closure in England.

WENDY. Thanks, Roger.

There's actually a lot of good news, Terry –

I can report fine weather and optimism after the World Health Organisation said that the NHS is one of the most cost effective health systems in the world. Across and up and down the country – babies have been safely born, diseases managed, health has been restored and lives have been saved.

But we're also looking at some very unsettled weather.

Let's have a closer look at the nationwide picture.

There's a severe cold front sweeping the north of England.

In Merseyside four thousand NHS jobs will go by the end of 2014.

In South Yorkshire Rotherham Hospital is set to lose seven hundred and fifty staff by 2015.

Greater Manchester's Trafford General Hospital – the birthplace of the NHS has had its A and E downgraded to Urgent Care. Salford Royal NHS Foundation Trust – staff cuts. Bolton NHS Trust – five hundred redundancies.

There is persistent pressure throughout London where at least seven A and E departments will close. In North-west London twenty-five per cent of beds to be cut. Up to five thousand, six hundred jobs will go.

In East Anglia – cuts.

In Exeter – cuts.

In Warwickshire – cuts.

Since the Coalition came to power over six thousand nursing posts have been cut.

So – we've got a combination of cuts and closures to hospitals – privatisation on the increase – PFI debts, waiting lists, stretched staffing levels and pressures on A and E.

The outlook is not all doom and gloom –

But should these patterns continue – it could create the perfect storm.

Scene Eleven

Bring on the Dancing Nurses

The Harrington. Geriatric Ward.

Babel at the hospital. The COMPANY *enter and engage in various activities, which culminates in a movement and choral piece.*

COMPANY. How are you feeling, Nancy? Can't you ring Chelsea and Westminster Hospital?

Bed-blocker.

Blockage transfer to neurology immediately.

MRSA. MRSA. MRSA.

Metastatic TCC bladder.

Scrub nurse and assisting nurse.

Shit piss and vomit must play a part.

Who the fuck did that?

Increased schizophrenia. Increased aggression.

Is it possible to get a cup of tea here?

Ward round.

Health and safety.

He needs to go to psychiatric.

Meet with the consultants.

Sort the chest infection first.

Periventricular brisk reflexes.

I'm going for a smoke. The importance of small things when you're on the edge.

Complaints about targets. Hospitals are bad places.

Cleaning bottoms.

Chemo was dripped through my body.

Nobody can find my notes.

They forgot to feed me.

It's the antithesis of the Hippocratic oath.

Hospitals kill.

I can't tell you how many patients I've killed.

The nurse did not acknowledge my mother's humanity.

I started working as a nurse at seventeen.

Every nurse is a potential killer.

Every doctor a swine.

This patient needs ECG.

All my life I dream of working for the NHS.

I went into medicine to play rugby.

Rise in demand for accountability.

The NHS has lost its way.

We've lost our NHS.

Who the fuck did that?

Scene Twelve

The Harrington. Geriatric Ward.

Two empty beds and one bed curtained off. DINAH (*an elderly patient*) *is talking to an empty chair. She chews constantly, open-mouthed – as if her mouth were dry. Her head hangs to one side.*

DINAH. A, b, c, d, s, t, u, v, amen. A, b, c, a, b, c, turn the telly off, amen.

A voice from the curtained area.

GINA. Come on, Mrs Dinah.

GINA exits the curtained cubicle. She closes the curtains carefully behind her.

Where are your slippers, Dinah? You'll get cold.

DINAH. A, b, c, amen.

MARIEL enters.

MARIEL. Excuse me.

DINAH crouches to pee.

GINA. Dinah? Dinah!

DINAH. Queen Victoria – sexy bitch.

MARIEL. Excuse me.

GINA (*to* MARIEL). Hello. (*To* DINAH.) Are you peeing?
Naughty.
No. Hold it in.
(*To* MARIEL.) I am Nurse Gina. How can I help you?

DINAH. That John Brown amen.

MARIEL. Where can I find Mrs James?
She arrived last night from A and E. I think it was bed seven.

DINAH. Amen. Amen.

GINA ushers DINAH away.

GINA. Ah. Yes, Dinah. Amen. Hold it in.
    I am washing her. Take a seat here.
    We weren't expecting you until later.

MARIEL. I'd like to see her.

GINA. Are you the next of kin?

MARIEL. Yes. I'm her daughter Mariel. My brother is on
    his way.

GINA. I understand.
    Are you okay, dear? Ahh. Get yourself a cup of tea if you
    like. I won't be much longer. There, there.
    Take a seat.

    She enters the curtained area. We hear her speaking.

    Now, dear. Is that all right? We just move you here. Mariel
    has arrived.

MARIEL. Hello, Mummy? I'll wait.

    GINA *pops her head out through the curtains.*

GINA. I just make Mamma nice for you.

    GINA *re-enters the curtained area.*

    Lift this leg. That's it. Well done.

MARIEL (*calling to* GINA). Can I assist with anything?

    GINA *pops her head out of the curtained cubicle.*

GINA. Is my job please.

    GINA *pops back inside.*

    MARIEL*'s mobile phone rings.*

MARIEL. Hello, Nicholas. Yes, take the lift to the sixth floor.
    Corridor on the right. Bed seven. Okay?

    GINA *pops her head out of the curtains again.*

GINA. Lady? Excuse? (*Points to the sign.*) No mobile phone.

    GINA *disappears behind the curtain again.*

MARIEL (*whispering*). I've just been told off. Okay.
(*Puts away her phone.*)

We hear GINA *talking behind the curtain.*

GINA. Sorry about that, dear. I'm going to just raise up your arm.
And then I'm going to turn you over.

ARCHIE *the hospital porter wheels on* JOHN, *a severe
stroke patient, to a bed opposite.*

ARCHIE. All right, sir?
Do you want to get into bed or stay in your limo?

JOHN. Baaaahhhhh.

ARCHIE. All right, pet. That's it. You're right. Best to sit up.

ARCHIE *helps* JOHN *to sit up a little straighter in his chair.
He gently puts a pillow under* JOHN'*s stroke-afflicted arm
and makes him comfortable.*

The nurse will be along in a bit. All right, my love?!

JOHN. Burrrr.

ARCHIE (*to* MARIEL). Are you being looked after, my love?
There's a coffee and tea trolley around the corner.
Tell them Archie sent you and they won't charge a penny.

MARIEL. I'm fine but thank you.

ARCHIE *exits.*

Hello.

JOHN. Ngggh humm – ph.

MARIEL. Sorry?

JOHN. Urrrrgggg – vaaa paaaa.

MARIEL *moves towards* JOHN.

JOHN *touches his mouth repeatedly.*

Urrrggg – vaa – paaa.

MARIEL. Do you want something?
A drink? A drink of something is it?

JOHN (*urgently*). Vaa urggg.

> *We hear* GINA *talking to the patient from behind the curtains.*

GINA. I'm going to roll you towards me, darling.

JOHN. Huuuuuup maa
Hup may
Hup. (*Gestures towards a table.*)

MARIEL. Shall I call a nurse for you?
Oh. You want the corn flakes. It's your breakfast is it?

JOHN. Gahh. Gay gayeshh.

MARIEL. I'll call a nurse.

GINA. And then we finish this arm, dear. Yes. Okay.

JOHN. Nahhh vayy ahhh.

MARIEL. Sorry. I can't feed you. I don't think it would be appropriate.
I'll call someone.

JOHN. Vayy vayyyyyyy.

MARIEL. Nurse? Nurse. Oh sorry –

> NURSE GINA *comes out of the curtained area and closes the curtains tightly.*

GINA. Mr John? You causing trouble again.

JOHN. Hupp hupp hupp may hadehh vayy.

MARIEL. I believe he wants his corn flakes.

GINA. Two ladies fussing over you. This is your lucky day.

JOHN. Hupp hupp nahhhh.

> *He strikes out at her.*

GINA. Are you raising your hand to me, Mr John? No.
Don't be cheeky. You're my old pal. Be a friend.

> *She holds his hands to calm him down.*

JOHN. Nahh vurgg.

GINA (*sings*). You are my sunshine. My only sunshine.
  You make me happy – when skies are grey.
  You'll never know dear how much I love you.
  Eat up all your corn flakes today.

*He takes one mouthful and chews a little – then he bubbles
and closes his mouth tightly.*

MARIEL. What happened to him?

GINA. He's had a very bad stroke poor man. It's not good is it,
  John?
  He's a vicar. Poor Reverend John.
  His wife doesn't want to know. She's in shock.
  (*Whispers loudly*.) She doesn't want him to come home.
  But – he's young. He may recover.

JOHN. Vayyy.
  Nayyy vayy.

GINA. Come on, Johnny. I don't have the time for this.
  Lots of patients wanting their wash.
  (*To* MARIEL.) Cold today.

MARIEL. Is my mother ready? I am very anxious to see her.

GINA. I absolutely understand but we wait please. I am in the
  middle of procedure. Rules and regulations.
  Come on, John. That's it. My sunshine.

JOHN. Bleuuu aaaahhhh hup.

He spits milk at her. GINA *checks him to make sure there's
no choking hazard.*

GINA. Okay. Feed yourself then. I'm gonna have to clean up
  now.

MARIEL. But I don't think he can – It's his breakfast.

GINA. He doesn't want it that badly.

  GINA *exits*.

JOHN. Hupp mayyy. Gah yeshh hep hep.

  MARIEL *looks around. She comes a little closer to* JOHN.

MARIEL. My name is Mariel.

JOHN. Fa ha. Hup, hup, vay gay yaaaaah.

MARIEL. Nice to meet you, John. I'm not supposed to do this
but –

*She picks up the corn flakes and carefully feeds him the rest.
She cleans his mouth.*

JOHN. Gayyy yeshh vayyyy urgggh.

MARIEL. Is that better? Well done. You poor old dear. You
were starving. Do you want some water?
Are the nurses terribly unkind? I will certainly complain on
your behalf.
I should like to do that for you. Oh, you poor dear.

JOHN (*whispers*). Vayyy.

MARIEL. Did you say something?

JOHN (*softer whisper*). Vah.

MARIEL comes closer.

He reaches out and grabs her breast.

MARIEL removes his hand.

MARIEL. You can't do that.

He grabs her again.

JOHN. Bahhhhh.

MARIEL. Owwww. Don't squeeze. You utter bastard.

JOHN. Furrdh jaaahhhh.

MARIEL. Reverend! Get your hands off me.

MARIEL wrenches herself free.

JOHN. Furrdh jahh. Fa ha. Fa ha. Aaaaaaahh.

MARIEL (*whispers loudly*). You should be ashamed of yourself.

*MARIEL adjusts her clothing and moves to the curtained
area.*

Mummy? It's Mariel. Are you decent?

GINA *returns and swiftly stops* MARIEL *entering*.

GINA. No. No, my dear.

MARIEL. Oh for goodness' sake. I am going to see my mother. Right now.

GINA. No. Mamma is not ready for visitors.

JOHN. Urgggghh.

GINA. Wait there please. Please.

GINA *goes into the curtained cubicle*.

MARIEL. What?

NICHOLAS *arrives*.

NICHOLAS. Hi. Where is she?

MARIEL. The nurse is washing Mummy – so I haven't actually seen her yet. In fact – she wouldn't let me.

NICHOLAS. Is that blood on the ceiling?

MARIEL *looks up*.

MARIEL. Probably arterial.

NICHOLAS. Good God.

JOHN. Faha. Furrdh jah.

NICHOLAS. In a communal room – the other end of the corridor is a bunch of what I imagine to be stroke victims in various states of catatonia. It's like a scene from *Awakenings*. Or the upstairs bar at The Garrick. I thought they got rid of mixed-sex wards.

MARIEL. You brought our mother here. You should have called me earlier.
I would have known where to take her.

NICHOLAS. Don't start, Mariel. I knew what to do. I did what Mum would have wanted.

MARIEL. Mummy was incapable of knowing what she wanted. She thought Ted fucking Heath was the Prime Minister. Do you actually want her to die?

NICHOLAS. Mariel, you look like a human being, but
    sometimes you don't sound like one.

MARIEL. Oh fuck off, Nick.

> MARIEL *calls out.*

> Excuse me. It's Gina isn't it?

JOHN. Urrgghhhh jayyyy.

> GINA *re-enters. She shuts the curtains tightly behind her.*

GINA. Yes.
    Patience is a virtue so the good book says.
    (*To* JOHN.) Does my nose tell me something? Have you
    done something? Why didn't you call me, Reverend?
    Then we wouldn't have this smell. Hmm?

MARIEL. You know there's blood on the ceiling.

GINA. Yes. It's been there for months.

NICHOLAS. Shouldn't somebody do something about it?

GINA. I don't know anybody tall enough.

JOHN. Vayyy.

NICHOLAS. We'd like to see our mother.

GINA. She is ready now. Are you the son? (*Whips off her
    rubber gloves.*)

NICHOLAS. Yes.

GINA. Doctor will be along presently.
    Someone is dying in Nightingale.
    Patient is patient.
    Yes. I'm so very sorry for all your troubles.

NICHOLAS. What troubles?

GINA. Doctor not tell you?

MARIEL. Tell us what?

NICHOLAS. We saw the registrar last night at about seven
    o'clock. My mother had recovered her memory by then.

GINA. I'm afraid Mamma died in the early hours.

NICHOLAS. Good God.

GINA. Her passing was very peaceful.

MARIEL. No. No.

GINA. Yes. Yes.

MARIEL. She was fine when we left her.

GINA. If you would like to see Mamma? Take a moment.

NICHOLAS. Our mother.
Nobody told us. She died last night?

MARIEL. I can't believe it. Oh, Nicholas. We're orphans. Oh
my God.

NICHOLAS. My God.

MARIEL. Mummy. Oh, Mummy.

They hold each other.

GINA. Come with me. I have made Mamma nice for you.

They enter the curtained area in a state of shock.

They come out in a further state of shock.

MARIEL. That's not my mother.

GINA. Yes, yes. I understand. It's hard to accept.

NICHOLAS. No, no. That's not our mother.

MARIEL. Where's Mrs James?

GINA. Mrs James?

ARCHIE *the porter wheels in* IRIS. *She is in good spirits.*

IRIS. Hello, darlings.

GINA. Ah. Why didn't you say Mrs Iris?
My dear, how are you?

IRIS. I'm very well, Gina. Thank you.
Nicholas – you're as white as a sheet.

NICHOLAS. I'm bloody glad to see you.

IRIS. You haven't shaved, Nicholas. We mustn't let standards drop.

NICHOLAS. Absolutely.

MARIEL *throws herself upon* IRIS.

MARIEL. Mummy.

IRIS. That's quite enough, dear.

NICHOLAS (*to* MARIEL). I've just lost ten years of my life.

MARIEL. So my mother isn't dead.

GINA. That's wonderful news.

IRIS. Of course I'm not dead.

MARIEL. But, but this is a complete cock-up – you said my mother had passed away.

GINA. Lady, you said bed seven.

NICHOLAS. Drop it, Mariel.

IRIS. What is she complaining about now?

MARIEL *expresses her frustration noiselessly.*

ARCHIE *and* GINA *help* IRIS *into a chair.*

GINA. Ahh. Mrs Iris is much improved. You're a lucky lady. You are no longer in the 1970s.

IRIS. They tell me I've had some kind of amnesia, but I can't remember a damn thing about it.

ARCHIE. Hope you get out today. Fingers crossed.

IRIS. Thanks for the spin, Archie, but I hope I don't see you again.

ARCHIE. Ha, ha. Likewise.

He wheels away the empty wheelchair.

NICHOLAS. The doctor wasn't entirely sure what was wrong with my mother.

GINA. Ah yes, yes, patient is patient. All variety of unusual things that might happen to us yes. Sometimes catastrophic.You had your CT scan?

IRIS. Yes.

MARIEL. What about an MRI?

GINA. We don't do that for the very elderly. Too expensive. Ahh, already Mrs Iris is a favourite. She wants to have a ward quiz. Sadly, most on this ward are – (*Whispers.*) incapacitated.

NICHOLAS (*to* GINA). So – the lady in there – who is not my mother – has been dead for some time?

GINA. Yes. Poor dear.

MARIEL. You were talking to her.

GINA. Regulations and protocol.
We must respect the patient at all times and talk to them.

NICHOLAS. Even when they are dead?

GINA. Especially when they are dead. Patient is patient.
Okay, Mrs Iris. Doctor gonna come see you very soon.

IRIS. Thank you, Gina.

NICHOLAS. How long will the deceased lady remain on the ward?

GINA (*shrugs*). Sir – don't even talk to me.
(*Whispers.*) Dead for hours before anyone noticed.
Bless you, Mrs Iris. We like Mrs Iris.
(*To* JOHN.) I'm coming back to you, my only sunshine.

GINA *exits.*

JOHN. Nayyy urggh vayyy.

NICHOLAS. You're looking so much better.

MARIEL. How are you feeling?

IRIS. A little confused if truth be known.
Was I gaga?

NICHOLAS. Lost to the fairies.

IRIS. A terrifying glimpse of the future.

MARIEL. Unlikely to happen again.

IRIS. I should jolly well hope not. The seventies is the last place
I want to spend my remaining days.
Someone tried to put a nappy on me last night. I threw it at
the nurse.
The bathroom is filthy.
There was a small stool in the shower tray and I don't mean
the three-legged kind. I refused to wash. I'm sure they have
me pegged as difficult seeing as most on this ward are gaga
waga. Oh dear, what's that smell?

NICHOLAS. It's poo, Mother.

MARIEL. Is it so hard to run a ward where the patients can
have a modicum of dignity?

JOHN. Blurrrg ma aunts.

MARIEL (*indicating to* JOHN's *bed*). The Reverend has
messed himself. Don't worry, Mum, I'm going to get you out
of here. Hank is making arrangements.

JOHN. Vayyyyyy.

IRIS. Don't you dare. I'm staying right here.

NICHOLAS. You asked me to bring Dad's letters.
Do you remember?

IRIS. No I don't, but I'm delighted. Did you think to bring my
glasses?

NICHOLAS. I did.

MARIEL. What letters?

From inside the cubicle we hear a low 'Wooooo
woooooooooooouuuuu'.

Nicholas – someone appears to be moving about in that
cubicle.

VOICE. Wooooooooooo oooooo.

DINAH *pops her head out of the curtain.*

DINAH. S, t, u, v.

IRIS. This is Dinah. We met last night.
In the early hours. When you screamed in my face.
Isn't that right, dear?

MARIEL. I'll call for a nurse.

DINAH (*aggressively to* MARIEL). Woo woooooo.

MARIEL. Right away.

MARIEL *moves off quickly to find a nurse.*

DINAH. We have lost the kingdom. Let's start a revolution.

IRIS. I see.

DINAH. I only want to do it with women.

IRIS. I beg your pardon?

DINAH. Bring the Government down. What a shower of bastards.
Crooks. Their hands are in my pocket. Get it out.

IRIS. A moment of clarity from Dinah. Do go on.

DINAH (*pointing at* IRIS). Mastermind.

IRIS. I like the idea.
But I don't want to be the mastermind.

DINAH. Me neither.

IRIS. You'll need to get some chaps involved. Ask my son Nicholas.

NICHOLAS. Don't encourage her.

DINAH. Anybody but that sexy bitch.

IRIS. Well, I suppose if you really want to do it I'll join in.
What should we do? Storm No. 10?

DINAH. Burn it down. Burn it.

MARIEL *returns.*

MARIEL. She's coming.

DINAH. I was a one. A sexy bitch. A Queen Victoria. You see
me now. My hair, my clothes. This body? You never know
what is going to happen to you. My husband was in the army
– then the police. We have children. Two children.
Grandchildren. So beautiful. Two and three. Dem say –
'Hello Dinah', on the telephone. Can you imagine? Only two
years old on the telephone? I was young. I was beautiful. I
was a sexy bitch. You never know what is going to happen to
you. You have a pretty face. Like a girl. Enjoy your life,
amen. Stick it in your family – album. Bum. Bum. Bum.

GINA *enters.*

Who will love me now?
A, b, c, d, s, t, u, v, amen. A, b, c, a, b, c, turn the telly
off, amen.

GINA. Yes, yes. I love you, Mrs Dinah. Come on now.

DINAH *slopes off like a sulky teenager.*

With two more geriatric wards closed – what are we to do
with these patients? Everybody needs attention.

JOHN. Gayhhhh yesshh harr.

GINA. Time for a wash, John.

JOHN (*cries*). Wahhhhhhhhhh.

*A buzz from a nurse alarm and cries of 'Nurse, nurse!'
from off.*

GINA *moves to* JOHN*'s cubicle. Further cries of 'Nurse,
nurse!' from off.*

Mr John? Don't move. I'll be back. (*Moves towards the
sound of the shouting.*)
(*Aside to the audience.*) We have three seriously ill patients
on this ward today.
If one of them goes off – I can deal with it – if all three go off
– I have to choose whose life to save. All my life in the UK I
want to work for the NHS but I didn't come into it for this.

A crash alarm sounds.

Here we go.

MARIEL. Let me know if I can be of help.

JOHN. Vuuuurgh ma aunts.

GINA. Yes, Mr John. You need cleaning – I know. I am
coming back.
Do not move.
Maybe keep a little eye on him?

GINA runs towards the sound of the alarm.

IRIS. She's really rather the nicest around here – but bonkers.
Absolutely bonkers.

*ARCHIE enters. He's wheeling an empty porter's wheelchair
and looking at notes.*

ARCHIE. Now.

He looks up and spots NICHOLAS *who has his head in his
hands.*

(*To the audience.*) Ah – bless him. He's very depressed. I
have to keep an eye on this one.
(*To* NICHOLAS.) There you are, sir. I was wondering where
you got to. So I'm to take you to physio, sir. Katie is waiting.
(*Attempts to get* NICHOLAS *to his feet.*) Come on, love.

NICHOLAS. I beg your pardon?

ARCHIE. Mr Paige? I hope you are not going to be difficult.

MARIEL. No, no. Check your list.

IRIS. This is my son, Nicholas.

ARCHIE. What? Oh sorry, love. Ha, ha, ha. Goodness me.
So – where is he? Oh dear, I've lost the patient. Hee, hee,
hee. Mr Paige? Mr Paige?

ARCHIE wheels off, whistling.

NICHOLAS. Did he think I was a patient? Did he?

Scene Thirteen

The Board of Directors Take Charge

All cast play board members – Chair, Chief Executive, Director of Nursing and Patient Experience, Chief Finance Officer and others.

The following is sung – three-part harmony.

ALL. The unexpected death of a surgical patient
    On the Morrison Ward
    Has been investigated
    And while root-cause analysis
    Has identified
    Some learning points
    The post mortem report states
    Death by natural causes.
    The formal inquest into this death has been listed for the
    25th of July.

    The unexpected death of an elderly patient
    On the Nightingale Ward
    Has been investigated
    And while root-cause analysis
    Has identified
    Some learning points
    The post mortem report states
    Death by natural causes.
    The formal inquest into this death has been listed for the
    30th of August.

    The unexpected death of a paediatric patient
    On the Hendell Ward
    Has been investigated
    And while root-cause analysis
    Has identified
    Some learning points
    The post mortem report states
    Death by natural causes.
    The formal inquest into this death has been listed for the
    30th of September.

DIRECTOR OF NURSING. Mr Chairman –

CHAIRMAN. Yes, Director of Nursing.

DIRECTOR OF NURSING. I would like to draw your attention
    to media coverage about our nurse staffing levels.
    They're being linked to the unexpected deaths.

ALL. By natural causes.

DIRECTOR OF NURSING. It's becoming a problem.

MATRON (*looking at figures*). There appears to have been
    a spike in staff turnover in the last six months –

DIRECTOR OF NURSING. – When we need to be hiring.
    Should we not discuss this –

ALL. At a future board meeting?

DIRECTOR OF FINANCE. Mr Chairman?

CHAIRMAN. Yes, Director of Finance?

DIRECTOR OF FINANCE. The good news is that we've made
    some savings –

DIRECTOR OF NURSING. On staff.

DIRECTOR OF FINANCE. And despite our continuing deficit
    we are still on course to achieve the statutory financial
    requirements to progress towards Foundation Status.

ALL. Hurray.

CHAIRMAN. Any further business?

DIRECTOR OF NURSING. Mr Chairman. I insist we put
    staffing levels at the top of the agenda for our next meeting.

CHAIRMAN. We'll put it immediately after salary review.

DIRECTOR OF NURSING. But we keep hiring expensive
    agency staff to cover the lack of our staff. It doesn't make
    any sense. We have to stop the cuts.

DIRECTOR OF FINANCE. You have misunderstood the NHS,
    the government, the needs of the community. Bland
    statements about stopping cuts won't guarantee the
    Harrington's future.

ALL. Sack her.

CHAIRMAN. The future is in our hands.

ALL. His hands.

DIRECTOR OF FINANCE. It's how it looks on the books
that counts.

ALL. Save money and balance the books.
Or we're cooked.
Completely fooked.

CHAIRMAN. Any further business.

ALL. No further business.

Scene Fourteen

Geriatric Ward.

IRIS *and* NICHOLAS *as before.*

HANK *enters.*

HANK. The cavalry has arrived.

MARIEL. Thank God.

IRIS. Oh fuck.

HANK. Nicholas.

    HANK *shakes* NICHOLAS*'s hand.*

NICHOLAS. Hank.

    HANK *embraces* IRIS.

IRIS. Oh for goodness' sake – Don't you both have a flight to
catch or something?
I thought Hank was supposed to give a paper this morning?

HANK. I've managed to change it until this afternoon.

MARIEL. Well done, darling.
We're not going anywhere, Mother.

IRIS. There's no need for you both to be here.

HANK. I've taken the liberty of booking an admission to the London Bridge Hospital. I hope you don't mind, Iris. They have a beautiful waterside room for you – If you so wish.

MARIEL. Hank has a colleague at the London Bridge, Mummy. A top neurologist.

IRIS. Yes. I heard.

JOHN. Fnaaagh. Mu ub hap ma.

HANK. They still have mixed wards here?

JOHN. Waaahrrg. Vurrrrrr ghaaaa.

MARIEL. John? What are you doing?

JOHN *tips himself out of his chair.*

JOHN. Ahhhhhhhgggg.

MARIEL. The Reverend is on the floor.

IRIS. Nicholas. Ring for the nurse.

MARIEL. Shit. I was supposed to be watching him.

MARIEL, NICHOLAS *and* HANK *go to* JOHN.

JOHN. Waahrrg. Vaaaaaa.

HANK. My name is Dr Questel. Sir? Are you hurt?

HANK *takes* JOHN*'s pulse.*

JOHN. Bleeeeeuugh.

MARIEL. He can't speak.

HANK (*checks for broken bones*). This place stinks. Dear God. Is that blood on the ceiling?
Honey, I don't think you'd mix up hospital and hotel here. This reminds me of the City Public where I worked as a junior doctor. It's where you go when you don't have insurance. I hate to think how many patients I killed there – by accident of course.
(*To* JOHN.) And how is that, sir?

JOHN. Fahhhhh haaaaa.

NICHOLAS. Is he okay?

JOHN *is crying*.

HANK. No broken bones. You're lucky, sir.

MARIEL. His name is Reverend John.

HANK. If you don't mind, Reverend John – Nicholas and I are going to help you off the ground.

NICHOLAS. Okay. What's the best way of doing this?

HANK. Lift him by the shoulders.

They start to shift him.

JOHN. Fahhhhh haaaaa.

They start to lift him. Shifting here and there. It's not particularly easy.

Gah vay bahhh.

MARIEL. I think you are hurting him?

NICHOLAS. He's a dead weight.

JOHN *ends up in an odd position*.

MARIEL. Come on. How hard can this be?

NICHOLAS. Do you want to lift him?

HANK. Where's the goddamn nurse?

HANK takes JOHN's pulse again. MARIEL shifts his cushion and adjusts him.

I think you gave yourself a bit of a fright, Reverend John?

JOHN. Gahhhh yesh.

MARIEL. There's a puddle of water. Be careful.

MARIEL grabs a handful of tissues and puts them on the ground.

IRIS. The poor fellow.

MARIEL. Don't worry, Reverend. Help is on the way.

HANK. Any sign of a nurse?

JOHN. Gahhhhhhhh.

GINA *enters*.

GINA. Okay, Mr John. What's going on?

JOHN. Hurappvvvh.

NICHOLAS. He fell out of his chair. We assisted him.

GINA. Mr John forgets he can no longer walk.
You moved the patient?

HANK. Nurse?

GINA. Gina.

HANK. Nurse Gina.
I'm an orthopaedic surgeon. I assessed this gentleman and
found no injury – though you will have to check for bruising.

GINA. If members of the public feel they must step in for staff.
That's it. I go. I'm going. Fuck this shit. They close the
wards, they cut the staff. I work for nothing. Fuck this
shitting fuck. Screw the bastards. I've had enough. Fuck this.
Fuuuucccckkk!

GINA *cries violently*.

HANK. There's really no need for that.

IRIS. Gina, we're terribly sorry. Aren't we, Hank?

MARIEL. Oh for goodness' sake.

IRIS. Shut up, Mariel. Hank?

JOHN *cries*.

HANK. I'm sorry if I've breached hospital protocol but I
couldn't leave the patient lying on the ground – particularly
in his condition.

GINA *recovers quickly*.

GINA. Patient is patient.
Mr John. Mr John. How many times must I tell you?
Now I'm going to have to fill out an incident form.

HANK. May I speak with Mrs James's consultant please?

DINAH *re-enters*.

GINA. Consultant is on the way.

JOHN. Burrrrrrr gah.

HANK. If you would tell him that Dr Questel of Cornell Hospital, New York, would like a word about a very important patient.

GINA. Dr Questel, in this country, patient is patient.
Mrs Iris is not an immediate priority as she is no longer in 1970. Now, visiting hours are from two p.m. until five p.m. So if you don't mind –

HANK. I don't think you understand.

JOHN. Vayyyy.

GINA. I understand that patient is patient.

HANK. Who is in charge around here?

DINAH. I am.

NICHOLAS. I'm becoming increasingly disturbed.

GINA. Sir, make an appointment with your GP.

NICHOLAS. There is blood on the ceiling and tissues of some description on the floor.

    DINAH *crouches to pee*.

GINA. Cleaning is outsourced. Take it up with the contractor. No, Dinah, naughty.

NICHOLAS. And there's a corpse some twelve feet away.

MARIEL. We were supposed to see a doctor at nine a.m.

DINAH. S, t, u, v, don't shave me.

HANK. We just want to know what is going on?

    GINA *comforts* DINAH.

GINA. No one is going to shave you, Mrs Dinah.

IRIS. It's only just gone ten o'clock.

GINA. I have been punched, kicked, spat at and that's just the relatives. Go complain. Call the CEO. Write to your MP. Ask how we go on without the staff. The desk is just there. On Your Way Out and by the way – welcome to your new NHS.

GINA *comes forward* (*holding* DINAH*'s hand*) *and talks to the audience.*

(*To the audience.*) Who am I supposed to tell that they don't like it?
The manager?
He cut the rota.
The board?
They cut the budget.
The press?
I get the sack.
Best to say that the 'Culture' is to blame.
Culture can't be sued. Culture can't be jailed.
Culture has nothing to do with Government policies.

THE GRIM REAPER *silently crosses the stage.* GINA *takes* DINAH *away.*

MARIEL. Mother. I want you transferred to a private hospital. Don't argue with me.

IRIS. You must be joking. They'll charge through the roof for scans and ECGs and will end up sending me back to the NHS because I'm too bloody old and banjaxed. I know how it works.

HANK. Mariel and I will pay for everything.

IRIS. It's not about money, Hank. I'm not moving.

NICHOLAS. Leave it, Mariel.

IRIS. The next thing – you'll be booking me into 'Autumn Lodge' or some such because 'you think it's best'. I'm not having it do you hear? Your father and I were there for the birth of the NHS.
We were amazed and grateful for Mr Atlee's brave new world. It's seen us through broken limbs, appendicitis, births and deaths. We've needed it and believed in it and I'm not going to stop now.
None of your generation know how to fight. You've never had to fight for anything. It's why we're all in this mess.

Now, you can all fuck off if you think I'm going anywhere.
Hank, go and give your paper. Go with him, Mariel.
Nicholas, you stay.
Where is that wretch of a doctor? This is all such a fuss
over nothing.

GINA *re-enters and sets up the blood-pressure machine
for* IRIS.

GINA. She's coming. Don't worry.
Everybody thinks they are expert.
Usual family fun.
Time for calming down.
I'm gonna take your blood pressure, Mrs Iris – so relax
your shoulder.

HANK. Darling, please don't cry.

JOHN *starts to cry. He outcries everyone.*

JOHN. Bahhhhhh ugggggghhhhhhhh.

MARIEL. I'm sorry. It's upsetting to see my mother here – in
this shithole.

NICHOLAS. She's certainly perked up a lot, Mariel.

GINA. Mrs Iris – have you drunk any water? You need to keep
up your fluids.

She pushes past HANK *and* MARIEL *and plumps up* IRIS*'s
pillows, feels her back and pours a glass of water.*

You're getting a little bit hot here ah?

MARIEL. If you'd like us to stay on I will cancel our flight
home.

IRIS. Dearest Mariel. I would hate you to cancel your flight.
Don't you worry.
I'd like to stretch my legs, Gina.

MARIEL. I'll take you, Mother.

GINA. Let me look after patient. You wait for doctor.
If Mrs Iris falls when you take her – I get sued. If she falls

when I take her I get sued. If she goes by herself and fall – I
get sued.

MARIEL. That's not going to happen.

GINA. It happens.

GINA *unstraps the blood-pressure monitor.*

Blood pressure a little raised – (*Looks accusingly at*
MARIEL.) but nothing too much to worry about. I write
for doctor.

IRIS (*as if* MARIEL *isn't there*). Have they gone, Gina?
I can't bear it.

GINA. Yes. They are leaving now.
(*Whispers loudly.*) Please go and get a tea or something.

GINA *ushers them to exit.*

MARIEL (*to* NICHOLAS). But you won't know what
questions to ask the doctor. (*To* IRIS.) Hank would be more
help than Nick.

NICHOLAS. I know what questions to ask.

IRIS. Yes, 'How long has she got?' That sort of thing.

HANK. Call me if you need help.

MARIEL. We will be back, Mummy.

MARIEL *and* HANK *exit.*

GINA. Okay, Iris?

IRIS. Come on, Gina.

GINA *and* NICHOLAS *assist* IRIS. NICHOLAS *hands* IRIS
her stick.

NICHOLAS. I will hold onto the doctor – if he ever gets here.

IRIS. If you recognise one. They all look about fifteen.

JOHN. Amanda.

GINA. Mr John!

JOHN. Amanda.

Scene Fifteen

A Man with a Plan

The PRIME MINISTER *and* MILTON, *his Campaign Strategist.*

MILTON. Prime Minister.

PM. They want to fire me, Milton.

MILTON. The public?

PM. The Party.

MILTON. We're changing that, mate. You're a man with a plan.

PM. Yes, I am.

MILTON. You're going to throw off your 'hug-a-hoodie' face
    for ever and come down like a ton of bricks.

PM. Jail-a-hoodie.

MILTON. You said it. Hit 'em.
    Hit hard from now on. Sometimes I think you wouldn't hit
    water if you fell off a boat but that's going to change. The
    problem with you is that you want to be liked.

PM. I want to be fair.

MILTON. You're not a fucking referee. You're the leader of a
    great country. People hating your guts comes with the
    territory, mate. Concentrate on the popular issues and leave
    green crap and the rest of it to the oppo.

PM. Tough on immigration.

MILTON. Tough – but fair – on immigration.

PM. Tough but fair on the economy.

MILTON. You've got to stop the Chancellor from smirking. It
    looks like he eats swan for lunch.

PM. I'll speak to him.

MILTON. Tough but fair on the Welfare State. Labour – The
    Welfare Party spent thirteen years letting the rot set in.

PM. We're busy putting it right.
    Rigorous with the NHS.
    Fuck – we're screwed on the NHS are we not?

MILTON. Mid Staffordshire happened on Labour's watch. Can
they defend the indefensible? Not a chance. Labour loosened
the screws for privatisation. Will the public forgive that?
Never!
We will turn their NHS record into a liability.
Mate, we are going to shoot their fucking knees off.

PM. On Labour's watch there was a thirty per cent reduction in
hospital mortality rates.
The targets worked, Milton.
I just can't see the medical fraternity allowing that record to
be completely rubbished.

MILTON. Prime Minister, come 2015 the public will have
heard so many bad-news stories they'll be begging you to
privatise. The medical fraternity will be too busy
resuscitating their image to defend Labour's record because
when we're through – every nurse will be a potential killer,
every doctor a lazy golfing swine and every patient about as
safe in hospital as a pig in an abattoir.

PM. And the public will be persuaded that Labour
systematically covered up Mid Staffs?

MILTON. It'll be as obvious as a dog's balls.
We've got measurements and figures we can work with.
Doesn't matter if the data is not quite accurate. Mud sticks.
People remember headlines not facts. The NHS will no
longer be safe in their hands.
But first let us unite even the most rebellious party members
in the main mission – the stonkering of Labour.

PM. Obliteration. Extinction.

MILTON. Good words.
Focus on Labour's weakness.
Red Ed still looks like a spineless union-loving seventies
throwback.
And by the time we have finished they will be unelectable
for decades.
You just need to keep drumming it through –
Labour did it.
If the economy dips? Labour did it.
If your hospitals collapse into bankruptcy? Labour did it.

If a hundred Bulgarians move into your street?
Labour did it.
If your dog gets run over?

PM. Labour did it.

MILTON. If your wife leaves you? Labour did it.
If there's a flood? Labour did it. Labour did it.

PM. The NHS collapses. Labour did it.

MILTON. And doctors and nurses did it. Lazy GPs did it.
We didn't do it. They did.
We have a strategy. We stick to it.

PM *and* MILTON. Labour did it.

Scene Sixteen

The hospital as before. JOHN *has regained a few words
of speech.*

He is crying. NICHOLAS *sits beside him.*

NICHOLAS. Don't cry. Your speech is coming back. That's
good, isn't it?

JOHN. Amanda. (*Cries.*)

NICHOLAS. Maybe I'll just leave you in peace?

JOHN. Amanda. (*Cries.*)

NICHOLAS. It's all right. It's all right.
I have some small understanding of how you might feel.
I lost my wife two years ago. I lost a job I loved.
It's a blow.

JOHN. Amanda.

NICHOLAS. But we're not finished yet!
Amanda is your wife, isn't she?

JOHN. God. Amanda.

NICHOLAS. I'm sure she'll come in to see you.

JOHN. God, God.

NICHOLAS. I am afraid of losing my mother. I'd be lost
without the old girl.
You and I need to resolve to keep going, keep fighting.

JOHN raises his arms to touch NICHOLAS.

NICHOLAS *comes closer so* JOHN *can rest his hand on*
NICHOLAS*'s shoulder.*

It seems like a blessing of sorts.

JOHN. Amanda. Amanda. Amanda, God. God.

NICHOLAS. Thank you.

GINA *and* IRIS *re-enter with* DR GRAY.

GINA. Ah, having a nice little chat with Mr John.

JOHN. Amanda.

IRIS. Look who we found.

DR GRAY. Good morning. Hello, John. My name is Dr Gray.
I'm the Consultant Physician here for the Department of
Health Care for Older People.

IRIS. Geriatric medicine you mean?

DR GRAY. Yes. Titles have a habit of going in and out of
fashion.

DR GRAY *and* NICHOLAS *shake hands.*

I'm sorry to have kept you waiting but there are some very
poorly patients on the ward. So – Mrs James... (*Peruses
the notes.*)

IRIS. Am I going senile?

NICHOLAS. Was it a stroke?

DR GRAY. No. Your scans were all fine.

NICHOLAS. So there's nothing to worry about?

DR GRAY. I spoke with the Professor of Neurology at Queens Square this morning and she advised that your symptoms seem classic for transient global amnesia – a rare condition of altered awareness. I'm afraid we know very little about TGAs except that they don't appear to be related to stroke at all. Few patients go on to have recurrent episodes.
It's just one of those things, Mrs James.

IRIS. I'm a medical phenomenon.

DR GRAY. We should monitor you in any case. I will organise an outpatient appointment for six months' time but given the possibility of hospital closure, it may have to be a community-based review. Is that all right?

IRIS. The Harrington will close you say?

DR GRAY. I hope not, Mrs James. Medical services have been delivered on this site since the fifteenth century.
I do want to keep you in for another night though.

IRIS. Oh shit.

DR GRAY. Your blood pressure is still a little high.

NICHOLAS. My sister wishes to move Mrs James to a private hospital.

IRIS. I'm not going.

DR GRAY. It's up to Mrs James.

IRIS. Thank you.
I've always thought the pursuit of profit to be bad medicine.

DR GRAY. I couldn't agree more.

NICHOLAS. Dr Gray, I am struggling with something.

DR GRAY. What is it, Mr James?

NICHOLAS. Why is this ward so understaffed?

IRIS. And there was a stool in the shower tray – it would be funny if it wasn't so disgusting.

DR GRAY. I'm truly sorry the service is not good enough.
I'm afraid we are suffering the effects of yet another

reorganisation. Happens with every new Minister of Health. It's like dogs with lamp posts. I'll make sure your complaint is heard.

GINA. Dr Gray – Can you come with me? I'm a bit worried about Reverend John.

DR GRAY. Please excuse me. I'll be back.

DR GRAY *moves away to talk to* JOHN.

ARCHIE. Still here?

IRIS. For another night.

ARCHIE. Oh dear.

GINA. Archie – they've turned the heating up –
Take 'you know who' to the morgue.

ARCHIE. Yes, ma'am.

GINA. I'll be back.

A distant crash alarm.

THE GRIM REAPER *crosses the stage.*

IRIS. Do you hear that?

NICHOLAS. I think it's a crash alarm in another ward.
Somewhere in the hospital someone is dying – poor soul.
Will I tell Mariel to come up from the canteen?

IRIS. Sorry?

NICHOLAS. Mariel and Hank – they are in the canteen. I should tell them to come up now?

IRIS. They live in New York. Where's Charles?

NICHOLAS. Mum?

IRIS. I think I'm losing my mind.

NICHOLAS. Dr Gray? Dr Gray!

GINA. Dr Gray is with Mr John.

NICHOLAS. Mrs Iris is having an episode of altered awareness.

IRIS. Where am I?

NICHOLAS. You're in hospital, Mother.

IRIS. What on earth am I doing here?

DR GRAY *enters*.

DR GRAY. Hello, Mrs James. My name is Dr Gray.
Gina? Blood pressure and sats.

IRIS. Where am I?

DR GRAY. You're in the Harrington Hospital.
And you are experiencing an episode of memory loss.
Can you tell me your full name?

IRIS. Mrs Iris Bethan James.

DR GRAY. And your date of birth?

IRIS. Seventeenth of the third nineteen twenty-three.

DR GRAY. Mrs James – can you raise your right arm for me?
And now your left?
Do these dates mean anything to you? 1066?

IRIS. Battle of Hastings.

DR GRAY. 1666?

IRIS. Great Fire of London.

DR GRAY. 1644?

IRIS. Battle of Marston Moor.

DR GRAY. What day is it today?

IRIS. Fuck knows.
What am I doing here?

NICHOLAS. You're in the hospital, Mother.

GINA. 160 over 90. Sats are fine.

DR GRAY. Who is the Prime Minister?

IRIS. It's not Ted Heath.

NICHOLAS. Great.

IRIS. It's Margaret Thatcher.

DR GRAY. You're confused, Mrs James.
Who is David Cameron?

IRIS. Does he play for Chelsea?

DR GRAY. Get Mrs James to Imaging please. She might be
embolising.
Ask Murdoch to join.

GINA. Yes, Dr Gray.

JOHN. God, God, God.

DR GRAY. I've not actually witnessed this before.

ARCHIE *exits the curtained area rolling out the bed with the
corpse.*

GINA. Archie? No. Leave that. We need to take Mrs Iris.

ARCHIE. Righty-ho.
Hello, Iris. Fancy a trip?

IRIS. Did we meet during the war?

ARCHIE. We met right here.

IRIS. Where is here?

ARCHIE. The Harrington Hospital.

IRIS. 1987?

ARCHIE. No, pet. It might feel like it but it isn't.

ARCHIE *rolls the bed back into the curtained cubicle.*

THE GRIM REAPER *walks across the stage.*

DR GRAY. We're going to find your memory, Iris.

IRIS. Oh dear. Am I losing my mind? Is it lost?

DR GRAY. Don't be frightened, Mrs James. We're going to do
our best to get it back for you. Gina, get Dr Shields from
Neurology to Imaging. She'll be very interested in this.

ARCHIE *begins to wheel* IRIS *off.*

IRIS. Nicholas? Nicholas? They're taking me away?
I haven't done anything.

DR GRAY (*to* NICHOLAS). Would you like to follow?

NICHOLAS. Yes of course.

IRIS. Where's Charles?

NICHOLAS *and* IRIS *exit*.

GINA. Reverend John is having a seizure.

DR GRAY. Put out a MET call, Gina.

GINA. Putting out a MET call.
(*Gets to a phone*.) Medical emergency on Cloudsley Ward.

Emergency beeps.

DR GRAY. John, John, can you hear me? It's Dr Gray. John?
It's okay.

A DOCTOR *runs on*.

STEPHEN. I'm Stephen – med reg. Is this the MET call?

DR GRAY. Yes. Are you comfortable doing an airway?

STEPHEN. Yes.

A SENIOR MATRON *enters*.

MATRON. Senior matron. What's the situation?

DR GRAY. Let's get him on the floor. This is a fifty-year-old
man admitted following a right-sided CVA with residual
weakness and expressive dysphasia, he started seizing
approximately two minutes ago. We are the first responders.
I will lead.

STEPHEN. One, two, three. I've got airway.

DR GRAY. I need someone on breathing.

STEPHEN *passes his stethoscope to* MATRON.

MATRON. I'm on it.

DR GRAY. Can you check he hasn't aspirated?

MATRON. Got it.

STEPHEN. Airway secure.

MATRON. Lung fields clear.

DR GRAY. John?
   Gina, take a blood pressure. John, can you hear me?
   Can someone prepare four milligrams of Lorazepam for slow
   IV infusion.

MATRON. Got it.

   MATRON *exits*.

DR GRAY. Change of plan. Can't get access. Can someone
   prepare ten milligrams IM Diazepam.

GINA. Yes, Dr Gray. 157 over 65.

DR GRAY. Okay. John? Can you hear me?
   Take a blood glucose level, Gina.
   Administering Diazepam.
   John? Can you hear me? John.

JOHN. Uhhhhhh.

GINA. Five point seven.

DR GRAY Seizure terminating. We need to get bloods.

GINA. On it.

DR GRAY. Let's get him straight to imaging for a CT scan.
   Good work, team.
   Welcome back, John.

Scene Seventeen

The Future of the Health Service

THE GRIM REAPER (*wheeling a bed*) *comes forward to speak to the audience.*

He shows the audience the deceased NHS *and then replaces the sheet over her.*

THE GRIM REAPER. Hello. I'm here to announce the demise of the NHS as you have known it. It has been a long, drawn-out illness that started when Margaret Thatcher came to power and with her a belief in the market, in consumer choice. Fast-forward to 2011 – the Coalition Government presented us with the Health and Social Care Bill, which became an Act and effective from April Fool's Day, 2013. This Act abolished the historic model of the NHS as a progressive tax-based system – delivered by public servants and paid for by all – instead you are being moved towards a US model and with that an NHS that does more with less, better, cheaper, faster – delivering a system of care that gives choice to patients and improves outcomes.
Picture the future –
State-of-the-art hospitals, polished floors, compassionate nurses, the concerned face of a consultant sitting at the bedside – no one ever makes a mistake – no one ever dies.

THE GRIM REAPER *winks at the audience.*

Let the good times roll.
I can't wait.

THE NHS. Where am I?

THE GRIM REAPER. Well, it's goodbye from her.

THE NHS. I'm not dead yet.

THE GRIM REAPER. Shaddup. (*To audience.*) I expect I'll be seeing all of you later.

Scene Eighteen

The main entrance of the Harrington Hospital.

Night.

NICHOLAS *is waiting.*

SAM. Oh hallo, sir! Pardon me. It's Constable Taylor. We met
   yesterday –

NICHOLAS. Yes. Of course, Constable. You were with, with a?

SAM. Prisoner. Yes, sir. Danny. Are you coming or going?

NICHOLAS. It's my mother.

SAM. Ohh! Sorry to hear it.

NICHOLAS. She's actually fine. She's going to be fine. I'm
   going home now.

SAM. Good news –
   No – I'm here because of Danny. Bad news. After his
   appointment yesterday he collapsed so they kept him in.
   Consultant says that the cancer has spread. Wildfire. Gone
   into his kidneys and liver – so, I'm afraid whatever they do –
   it's looking like curtains – could be only – days...

NICHOLAS. Oh no – that's awful. I'm so sorry.

SAM. Yeah, I was fond of the old bugger – it's a bit of a shock.
   Still, it'll save the Government the cost of another couple of
   years inside.
   He asked me to get Maggie.

   SAM *uncovers the birdcage and* MAGGIE *chirps.*

   Maggie.

NICHOLAS. That was kind of you.

   Maggie.

   A car horn.

SAM. Thing is I'm not allowed to bring Maggie up to the ward
   in case she gives everyone budgie flu – health and safety –

you know. I've got to bring Danny down to the front
entrance. So, I was wondering, if you'd hold on to her for
about ten minutes?

NICHOLAS. Of course. But that's my taxi.

SAM. Not to worry, sir. I'll figure it out.

NICHOLAS. No, no. Please. I'll tell the driver to wait. Just give
me a moment.

He exits.

BEVAN *and* CHURCHILL *pull their greatcoats about them
and step forward.*

BEVAN. We'll hold on to Maggie for you, Officer. Off you go.

SAM. Much obliged, sirs. I won't be too long. (*Exits.*)

CHURCHILL. I am very fond of budgerigars.
Hello, old girl.
I taught mine to speak.

BEVAN (*to* MAGGIE). Hello. Hello. Hello.

CHURCHILL *and* BEVAN *both coo and make noises at*
MAGGIE.

CHURCHILL. It made me very sad to be old. Old age is
intolerable. How distressing to spend one's last breath in
such a place.

BEVAN. Under the vandals' stewardship the Health Service has
become like Lavinia in *Titus Andronicus* – all the limbs cut
off and eventually her tongue will be cut out, too.
The clock is being turned back, Mr Churchill. Or at least –
that is what the vandals are attempting to do.

CHURCHILL. On the contrary – after decades of paralysis we
are going forward, Mr Bevan, and British enterprise will
finally be allowed to flourish. Wards such as we've seen shall
be a thing of the past. And I believe we have the full support
of the public because if the people were afraid of losing their
precious NHS to so-called vandals – then, Mr Bevan – they
are keeping very, very quiet about it. No, sir, you'll find they
are reassured.

NICHOLAS *re-enters*.

BEVAN. They do not understand what is happening, Mr Churchill. People who live in mountainous and rugged countries are always afraid of avalanches, and they know that avalanches start with the movement of a very small pebble. It starts on a ridge between two valleys and if nobody bothers about the pebble – it gains way, and all too soon the valley is overwhelmed. That is the logic of the present situation. The pebble is gaining way.

CHURCHILL. Change is rolling in. Let it roll. It must roll on full flood to better days.

NICHOLAS. But who do we look to now?

CHURCHILL. Good question. Isn't that right, Maggie?

MAGGIE *chirrups*.

BEVAN. The people are reacting sharply to this wholesale destruction. No political party that attempts to destroy the Health Service can hope to command the support of the British people. Look to the people. It is they who must demand political courage.
They must fight for a Health Service that protects them.

MAGGIE. We should not expect the State to appear in the guise of an extravagant good fairy at every christening, a loquacious and tedious companion at every stage of life's journey, and the unknown mourner at every funeral.

CHURCHILL. Good God, it's Margaret.

This location goes to dark and we return to IRIS *on the ward.* GINA *is looking after* IRIS *and making her comfortable.*

IRIS. The ward is so quiet without poor Reverend John. But you and Dr Gray saved his life.

GINA. Yes, yes. He's doing fine. Reverend John has fighting spirit. He wants to live.

IRIS. Marvellous. (*Takes off her glasses and rubs her eyes.*)

GINA. Come on, Mrs Iris. You're tired aren't you? Bedtime.
It's been an upsetting day.
Do you want to go the bathroom?

IRIS. That's very sweet but haven't you finished for the day?

GINA. All in a day's work.
I'll put these letters away for you.
Ooh – the writing is small – isn't it? Faded pages.

IRIS. It was written in March 1939. Some six months before the
Second World War broke out.

GINA. From your husband?

IRIS. Yes.

GINA. Did he fight in the war?

IRIS. Oh yes. He got an MC at Dunkirk.

GINA. I don't really know much about the Second World War.
Is Mr James still with us?

IRIS. He died nearly twenty years ago. I miss him so very
much. In the months before he died he took to studying old
road maps – I wondered why until I realised he was tracing
his retreat to Dunkirk.
Perhaps I am tracing my own journey –
You know, he was one of the last members of the 1940
expeditionary force to leave France?

GINA. We're not supposed to hug the patients – but would you
like one?

IRIS. I don't think one would be out of the question.

GINA *gives* IRIS *a squeeze.*

GINA. There now. Come on, lovely.
We'll go to the bathroom.
Ah – when it's still and quiet – it's wonderful.

She pushes the wheelchair as if to go.

IRIS (*suddenly she grips* GINA*'s hand*). Gina.

GINA. Everything okay, Mrs Iris?

IRIS. We must not give up, Gina. We must fight.
There is still time.

GINA *pushes the wheelchair to exit.*

NHS SOS: How the NHS Was Betrayed – And How We Can Save It

'Since 2000, Governments have pursued a policy for the NHS that the electorate hasn't voted for and doesn't want'. *

If you are alarmed and angry after seeing – or reading – this play you should be. No one voted for the market-driven policies that are being forced on the NHS, there is no democratic mandate for them. Indeed in 2010 David Cameron promised that there would be 'no more of those pointless NHS reorganisations that... bring chaos'. Shortly after the Coalition came into power he began to legislate for a reorganisation so large that it could, according to the NHS CEO Sir David Nicholson, be seen from outer space.

We are already seeing the disastrous consequences with fragmentation of the service, unaccountable private providers pulling out when they can't make profits, the NHS budget wasted on compulsory tendering and litigation. Caught up in this are the patients and the staff whose voice, far from driving the agenda as promised, has all but disappeared.

How was it allowed to happen? The NHS is the most popular institution in the country, and Bevan was right when he said that no political party would survive that tried to destroy it. So politicians have had to work behind closed doors to transform it from an integrated public service into a Kitemark attached to competing private providers. They have peddled myths about it – we can't afford it, it can't go on like this – which are demonstrably untrue but are swallowed by the media. They have lied about its cost and its outcomes. They have used language – patient choice, modernisation, plurality of providers – which has concealed their true agenda. They have always denied accusations of privatisation.

Thanks to this toxic mix of spin, bogus public consultations and outright lies, the last pieces of the jigsaw are falling into place and the NHS as we have known it – publicly funded, publicly delivered and publicly accountable – now stands on the

---

* *The Plot Against the NHS* by Colin Leys and Stewart Player (Merlin Press Ltd, 2011)

brink of extinction. But the NHS belongs to us, the public, and it is up to us to do something about it. It is not too late. There are things that we can do and there are things that we can press politicians to sign up to. So don't get mad, get active. Here are some ideas as to what you might do:

Firstly you can't fight alone so join up with others. Join an established campaign like Keep Our NHS Public (KONP), which has local campaign groups. If there is no group near you, think of starting one; KONP will help with material and speakers. There are also many campaigns organised around local problems such as hospital cuts and closures. All these local and national campaigns are starting to work together for greater effect. Many other organisations such as the NHS Support Federation give guidance about how to campaign, links to national campaigns are listed on page 91.

We need to track the changes to the service – much of what is happening, including financial dealings and patient outcomes, is being lost behind a smokescreen of 'commercial confidentiality'. Groups can monitor proposed local changes, be they cuts, closures or outsourcing of NHS services. There are at least two sites where cuts, closures and privatisation are being collated, visit them to provide and get information. And stay informed – the Government's greatest ally is apathy, ignorance and fatalism about what's happening. There's a suggested reading list below, and Twitter users can get up-to-date news by following the Twitter feeds of the listed organisations.

We must persuade politicians that the NHS will be a massive issue at the General Election in 2015. Write to your MP and tell them that, especially if they are Tory or Lib Dem, organise local hustings to question them. Labour also needs to be reminded that we care about the NHS. They have already committed to repealing the Health and Social Care Act (HSCA), but they can also promise to support Lord Owen's Bill to restore the responsibility of the Secretary of State to deliver the NHS, something that the Act abolished for the first time in sixty-five years.

There are many other ways that groups can influence what is happening. Firstly they can act within the structures of the NHS, although the patient voice has been much weakened. Members of the public can attend CCG board meetings, become governors on Foundation Trust boards, join or start patient participation groups at their local surgeries. Most GPs are horrified at what is happening and are likely allies, talk to them about putting campaign material in their waiting rooms.

Groups can help inform and mobilise public opinion with local street stalls, marches, petitions and such like. Some people will be comfortable with writing letters, others talking to the local media, who are another natural ally. If the media fail to cover an important story, complain to them.

Most importantly, don't lose heart. People across England are now waking up to the dismantlement of the NHS, a project that benefits no one but the private sector. Aneurin Bevan said, 'The NHS will last as long as there are folk left with the faith to fight for it.' We believe those folk are out there and are ready to fight.

A more detailed version of this advice on action can be found in the last chapter of the book *NHS SOS*.

Jacky Davis,
Founder member of Keep Our NHS Public,
Chair of the NHS Consultants Association,
Consultant radiologist (London)

National Campaigns
Keep Our NHS Public (www.keepournhspublic.com)
London Health Emergency (www.healthemergency.org.uk)
NHS Support Federation (www.nhscampaign.org)
National Health Action Party (www.nhap.org)

Allied Organisations
Centre for Health and the Public Interest (www.chpi.org.uk)
NHS Consultants Association (www.nhsca.org.uk)
Open Democracy (www.opendemocracy.net/ournhs)
Spinwatch (www.spinwatch.org)

Suggested Reading and Watching
*NHS SOS: How the NHS Was Betrayed – And How We Can
   Save It* by Jacky Davis and Ray Tallis
The Plot Against the NHS by Colin Leys and Stewart Player
NHS Plc: The Privatisation of Our Health Care
   by Allyson Pollock
Health Policy Reform: Global Health Versus Private Profit
   by John Lister
Myth-busting the NHS
   (www.redpepper.org.uk/mythbuster-health-warning)
*Privatising the World: A Study of International Privatization in
   Theory and Practice* by Oliver Letwin
Spinwatch on health lobbying
   (www.youtube.com/watch?v=WDj-1D6U0LU)
The Spirit of '45 by Ken Loach

Other Titles in this Series

A Nick Hern Book

This May Hurt A Bit first published in Great Britain as a paperback original in 2014 by Nick Hern Books Limited, The Glasshouse, 49a Goldhawk Road, London W12 8QP, in association with Out of Joint and Octagon Theatre Bolton

This May Hurt A Bit copyright © 2014 Stella Feehily

Stella Feehily has asserted her right to be identified as the author of this work

Cover image © Martin Rowson

Designed and typeset by Nick Hern Books, London
Printed and bound in Great Britain by CPI Group (UK) Ltd

A CIP catalogue record for this book is available from the British Library

ISBN   978 1 84842 359 6

www.nickhernbooks.co.uk

 facebook.com/nickhernbooks

 twitter.com/nickhernbooks